Christopher's Contemporary Catechism

19 Sermons Answering 25 Questions from the Pews

By Chris Halverson

Christopher's Contemporary Catechism: 19 Sermons Answering 25 Questions from the Pews
Copyright © 2016, Christopher Lee Halverson, all rights reserved
Cover Art by Kristin Walker
All rights reserved.

A special thank you to St. Stephen Lutheran, South Plainfield, NJ for giving me my first five years of ordained ministry!

Why a Contemporary Catechism?

Even if you never had to memorize Luther's Small Catechism, you probably remember one of the most common phrases found inside, "What does this mean?"

One of the apocryphal stories about this question is that Luther's son, Hans, constantly asked this question of Luther every time he theologized too far into the clouds. The Lutheran faith became grounded in answering this boy's questions.

In a similar vein, I started up a summer sermon series—20 Questions in 10 weeks. It seemed to me that one of the dangers of preaching every week from the lectionary was that my theology could miss the mark, not because it was wrong, but because it could get too far into the clouds. And so the members of St. Stephen humored me the spring before I started this series by filling our question box with question. In doing this they helped plant my preaching on firm ground.

The first year was so well received I did it a second and third year, ending up with 19 sermons total. 19 sermons applying Lutheran Theology and my own pastoral sensibility to 25 questions from my congregation. I hope and pray our wrestling with these questions may be helpful for you, dear reader.

Year 1
1. Cross and Communion
2. Angels and Demons
3. Calendar
4. Gay Marriage
5. The Law and Christian Life
6. Reward, Equality, Baptism
7. Suffering and Death
8. Sin and Forgiveness

Year 2
9. The Trinity
10. Sacrifice and Self Care
11. Salt, Light, and Hands
12. Foreknowledge, Predestination, and Human Will
13. Church Attendance
14. Religious violence
15. Holocaust and Lutheranism
16. The End

Year 3
17. Samson's Faith
18. Easy Sin, Hard Faith
19. Justice

Year 1

1. Cross and Communion
(Matthew 26:26-30)

This summer I'm going to be preaching a little differently—I'm going to be preaching **topically**, specifically on topics related to questions the congregation submitted to me during the last month. This sermon series began last week when Pastor Jim answered questions about the Lord's Prayer and Discerning God's Will.

Today I will be preaching on two questions:
1. What is the significance and meaning of the procession of the cross at the beginning and end of the service?
2. Do we as Lutherans believe the bread and wine literally change into Jesus' body and blood? I assume different Protestant sects believe different things in this regard. I believe Roman Catholics do believe it changes.

I will tackle these questions bit by bit. First I will deal with the procession of the cross into church and then we will process the cross into the worship space here today
Next, during the typical time of the Sermon I will tackle the communion question.
Then, finally, before the recession of the cross, I'll cover the significance of recessing the cross.

Procession
We process in with the cross in order to acknowledge the symbol of our redemption—the Cross of Christ. We remember the life giving act of God's son for our sake, his death on the cross.
By beginning the service in such a way, we remind

ourselves what kind of community is gathered here. It is a cross shaped community, a community immersed in Christ's death, and made alive with Christ in his resurrection.

Entering with the cross reminds us that we are a community defined by our Baptism into that death and resurrection of Jesus.

That in fact, is why the next thing we do in worship, after processing with the cross, is that we return to the font, where we were Baptized, either through confession and forgiveness like we will do today, or in a more literal sense with Thanksgiving for Baptism.

We process the cross to remind ourselves we are a cross people.

Communion

The official Lutheran answer to the question asked today about communion can be found in the Smalcald Articles as well as in Luther's Large and Small Catechism.

In the Smalcald Articles it is written:
"Concerning transubstantiation, we have absolutely no regard for the subtle sophistry of those who teach that the bread and wine surrender or lose their natural substance and that only the form and color of the bread remain, but it is no longer real bread. For it is in closest agreement with scripture to say that bread is and remains there as St. Paul himself indicates "The bread that we break" and "Eat of the bread."

And yet, we also affirm the words of Luther's Large Catechism:
"It is the true body and blood of the Lord Christ, in and

under the bread and wine, which we Christians are commanded by Christ's words to eat and drink... the sacrament is bread and wine, but not mere bread and wine such as is served at the table. Rather, it is bread and wine **set within God's Word and bound to it.**"
"It is true, indeed, that if you take the Word away from the elements or view them apart from the Word, you have nothing but ordinary bread and wine. But if the Words remain, as is right and necessary, then by virtue of them the elements are truly the body and blood of Christ. **For as Christ's lips speak and say, so it is**; he cannot lie or deceive."

So, what's going on here? Luther is threading the needle between two different understandings of the Lord's Supper which rely on Logic instead of Faith.

In the first case, Luther is standing against Medieval Roman Catholic understandings of the Lord's Supper, which rely on the science of the time, Aristotelian Logic, in order to explain what happens during communion.
This way of looking at communion makes the claim that we are assured that Jesus is present with us in communion, **because all things in the universe have accidents and substance.** The accident of the thing is that which can be seen, touched, felt, etc, and the substance of the thing is what the thing actually is.

So, for example, a fun joke you can play on your friends when you are in the hospital, is to get **a Urine Sample Cup**, fill it with apple juice, and drink it in front of them.
In that case the accident is Urine, but the substance is Apple Juice.

Just so, Medieval reliance on Aristotilian Logic insists we know Jesus is in communion because bread and wine are the accident and flesh and blood are the substance.

Luther hears this argument and says, "That's all math to me... we should believe Jesus is truly present in communion because he truly promises to show up, and Jesus doesn't lie."

In the second case, Luther is standing against other protestant reformers like the French John Calvin and Swiss Huldrich Zwingli. They too, he felt, clung to logic instead of faith.

When they debated with Luther about the Lord's Supper they clung to a literal understanding of scripture—specifically that Jesus is at the Right Hand of the Father... which to them meant Jesus clearly couldn't show up in bread and wine here on earth, because he was up in heaven.

Luther countered that The Right Hand is a Hebrew way of saying strength or power, and so the Traditional understanding of that power involves the ubiquity of Christ—at essence, Jesus isn't bound to any one place.

For example, if you read the end of several of the Gospels, Jesus walks through walls, shows up on the road to Emmaus, and so on. So clearly he's not stuck on a cloud somewhere, clearly he can show up in bread and wine if he promises he is going to.

So convinced was Luther of the real presence that he met with Zwingli in Malburg and they went round after round for days and days about the real presence that Luther began to etch into the table they sat at "Est ist est." That is "Is means Is."

As I read in the gospel today Jesus says, "this IS my

body" and "this IS my blood."

So the question quickly becomes, why isn't this common knowledge among Lutherans?

To paraphrase the eminent theologian Mel Brooks: "I blame the Irish."

During the American Civil War tons of Protestants were dying left and right, just as Immigration from Catholic Ireland was picking up.

And Samuel Schmucker, a Princeton Grad and one of the founders of The Lutheran Theological Seminary at Gettysburg, saw this and lost his head. He believed the only way to keep Roman Catholicism from taking over America was to join Lutheran Protestants with Calvinist Protestants by chucking our understanding of Holy Communion.

In response to this move away from traditional Lutheranism, a cadre of Faculty left Gettysburg and started up a new seminary in 1864, the Lutheran Theological Seminary at Philadelphia.

Similarly, Lutherans in parts of the country in which everyone is either Lutheran or Catholic—especially in the Midwest—tend to downplay or even misrepresent our understanding of Communion in order to make a greater distinction between us and our Roman neighbors.

But that's all a lot of history and maybe a little dry. The important thing to know is this, **Jesus shows up in the meal, he is really present. We know this to be true because he promises to show up, and Jesus doesn't lie!**

If your beloved promised to meet you at the train station, would you sit at home wondering if mathematics can prove her arrival? Would you spend your time fretting over how she made it to the train station? No, you would run stop lights to get there and see her!

So too with Jesus, he promises to meet us in the meal! Rejoice, he will be there! Rejoice! His words point us to the reality of his forgiveness—in the meal Jesus promises us forgiveness, life, and salvation. A+A

Recession

When we recess with the Cross, we find ourselves between the rich meal of Communion and the cross of Christ.
Fed and now following, bringing with us that promise we received in the Body and Blood of our Lord, to be shared with a hurting, crucified, world.

We are led out into the world to find God in unexpected places, God on the cross, following Christ wherever he may lead.
A+A[1]

---

[1] A+A=Amen and Alleluia

2. Angels & Demons
(Daniel 10:10-14, Mark 5:1-20)

Just to remind everyone, as a summer sermon series I'll be preaching topically. Specifically, I'll be preaching on questions that you all have submitted over the last month.

Today, both questions are questions involving spiritual beings. They are:
1. What's the deal with Angels? Do humans become angels when we die?
2. Is there a particular significance to Jesus casting the Legion of Evil Spirits from the Gerasene Demoniac into a herd of swine?

Let us pray:

To start off with, when we talk about Angels it's important to admit right off the bat that they are mysterious.
For example, in the book of Genesis various patriarchs run into what appears to be a human messenger, then they describe it as an Angel, then sometimes it becomes the Angel of the LORD, then finally it is described at God!
Clearly something odd is happening.
Likewise, if you read the book of Ezekiel you'll find Angels who are things, for example pieces of God's throne, and elsewhere angels described simply as "flaming things."
All that to say, they're strange things and I'm clearly not going to nail down what they are, but we can at least take a few swings at it.

Tackling the second half of the question before the

first, there is nothing in scripture that indicates humans become angels when we die.

The closest we come to an actual example of a human becoming an angel is one non-canonical
—meaning from writings which are not considered scripture
—one non-canonical instance in which Enoch,
remember Enoch, the guy who walked with God and then was not—Noah's great-grandfather...
well, there is a tradition in which Enoch is "translated" into an angel named Metatron.

That said, there is a larger Pastoral concern behind the question, there is a bigger question being asked, which is:
"Is there still a connection between me and my dead loved one?"

And to that I respond yes.

We are held fast by the One Who Was, Who Is, and Who Will Be, the one who transcends time and has conquered death.

Each Sunday we eat together before the altar, at a meal that anticipates the destruction of death and the wiping away of all tears,
anticipates this great culmination, (here's the kicker) which has already happened through Jesus Christ.

So, when we kneel before this half-circle altar rail... half-square actually... we can be confident that the invisible other half of the railing around the altar is filled with our sisters and
brothers who were and who will be.

As to the other half of the first question, what are

angels?

There are a lot of different ways to think about the nature of angels, I'm just going to briefly give you two I think can be helpful.

The first comes from Augustine's City of God. He reads the creation of light on the first day in Genesis chapter 1 as the creation of angels as "partakers of the eternal Light which we call
the only-begotten Son of God."

As for the darkness, Augustine writes, "If an angel turns away from God, he becomes impure," an unclean spirit.
Essentially angels are like the moon, they are beings who reflect the light of Jesus Christ, and when that light is eclipsed they become evil.

Now, the interesting thing that comes out of this meditation upon Angels and Demons is that he affirms, "Evil has no nature of its own. Rather, it is the absence of good, which has received the name evil."

This is probably one of the most powerful realizations in all of Augustine's works—evil isn't a thing, it is simply the absence of good! The dark side of the moon isn't defective, it simply needs to reflect the light of the sun!
Imagine what this means for our redemption!

For the second way to think about angels we need to fast forward 1600 years or so from Augustine to a guy with the funny name Walter Wink.

Dr. Wink wrestled for years and 100's of pages with the question "what are these spiritual beings?"—Angels, Powers, Heights, Depths—all those things which Paul writes can not separate us from the Love of God in Christ

Jesus.

And it was in reading Daniel that Dr. Wink hit upon an in to understanding the Spiritual Powers. The angel who comes to Daniel was slowed down by the Prince, the Angel, of Persia. Dr. Wink thought through the meaning of particular nations having Angels assigned to them, and concluded these Spiritual Powers are (dis?)embodiments of those things which no one person controls.

So, for him, Spiritual Powers are almost like the ethos of corporations, nations, places, etc.

And, he goes on to point out, like all created things, they are fallen and in need of redemption... in fact this is one of the tasks of the Christian faith.

His main example is the end of Apartheid in South Africa. By seeking a non-violent solution to the transition of power in that country, through Truth and Reconciliation, the Spiritual Ethos of South Africa was redeemed—an exorcism of Apartheid was done to that country.

Let's take this way of looking at Angels and other Spiritual Powers and bring it a little closer to home:

About two weeks ago some of us got together and began to explore what hunger looks like in the US, and we were overwhelmed with how many moving parts there were, and that some things being done to alleviate hunger actually weren't doing much good.

The systems in place in this country to feed people well, are out of whack—Walter Wink would say this is actually a Spiritual problem, these systems which are bigger than any one person are in fact tied to a Spiritual Power and that Power is sick, if not demonic, and therefore it is our duty as Christians to try to, through non-violent self-giving acts, redeem that system so it once again functions as God intended it to.

And finally, in a very round about way, that gets us to the question about Legion. Notice the demons are named Legion—the same name as Roman Legions, the army, who occupies Israel.

If an army, a thing bigger than any one person, had an Angelic sense to it, it would be one which focused on defending the weak and needy (this is why Luther recommend that we ask for God's Angels to Defend us), yet Roman Legions occupied Israel making its population weak and needy—this is a perversion of God's intentions, it is Demonic.

This person, whose home is occupied by Roman Legions (or alternatively is himself a cast-away member of a Roman Legion), is occupied by unclean spirits named Legion. The physical reality is being manifest in a spiritual way.

And so Jesus decolonizes this man's Spirit, and the colonizing power, Legion, doesn't want to be kicked out of the land currently being occupied by the Roman Legions (see verse 10). So Jesus sends an unclean spirit into an unclean animal, a swine.

In summary:
1. Jesus finds an unclean place for an unclean thing.
2. Reflecting upon the nature of Angels help us
a) think about redemption as a passive reflection of the good light of
Christ, and that
b) redemption can involve the spirit of whole systems.
3. Finally, we don't become angels when we die, but we can trust that
all the Saints of God—both living and dead—are one in Christ Jesus.
A+A

3. Calendar
(Genesis 2:1-3, Deuteronomy 5:12-15, and Exodus 31:15)

As we continue on our summer sermon series, <u>20 questions in 10 weeks</u>, today's questions both touch on the topic of **calendar**.

The first is:
"What Season was Jesus born? Fall, Winter, Spring, or Summer?"
And the second is:
"Why do people go to church on the Sabbath?

Let us pray.
On the face of it, the question "What season was Jesus born?" seems a little odd. When I asked a colleague about it, his response was, "This is like asking what color Christ's hair was... the actual answer can only matter if we've prioritized something that doesn't matter as though it does."

But, I looked around a little, just to see where people go with this question, and found out there is a lot of arguments against celebrating **Christmas** that start with the question "What season was Jesus born in?"

So here's how the logic of these arguments go: "Oh, of course Jesus was born in the Winter."
"That's impossible, the shepherds had sheep outside, and it is *too* cold in the winter to have sheep outside.
For that matter, no Emperor would hold a census in winter, because he wouldn't want to be *cruel* to his subjects!
And it would be *so* cold that the Virgin Mary would have frozen to death and Jesus would never be born.

And so clearly Christmas is actual the Pagan practice of worshipping the Sun's birth on "Sol Invictus."

So, a few things to consider about this argument:
Firstly, every person who makes this argument cites Adam Clarke, an Irish academic from the 1800's. Now the little village Clarke lived in was kinda cold in December, between 45 and 36 degrees. But, Bethlehem averages between 57 and 45 degrees in December, not swimming weather, but it's not going to kill you either.
Secondly, Roman Emperors were cruel from time to time.
Thirdly, there was no formal recognition of this type of worship of the sun until 274CE, 72 years after the death of Irenaeus, the first recorded Church Father to suggest December 25th as Christ's birth.

But I agree with my friend, arguing about this type of thing is majoring in the minors, and not really the Lutheran way of doing faith, but I'd imagine that would help the questioner think about the date of Christmas a little more.

The more interesting of the two questions, at least to me, is: **"Why do people go to church on the Sabbath?"** And spreading the question out a bit: **what's the Sabbath for?**

Reading in exodus we see a very severe accounting of Sabbath—it's about **rest** and **holiness**... and if you don't do it you are to be put to death.
In Genesis and Deuteronomy we get two sources of this command.
From Genesis we see the Sabbath is **holy** on

account of being associated with God's holy act of **creation**, and Sabbath is about **rest** because on the 7th day **God rested**.

From Deuteronomy we read that the Sabbath is **holy** because of **God's liberation of his people from Slavery into Freedom**, and it requires **rest** because a people who were once slaves **should not let anyone in their society live in the slave-like condition of constant labor**.

And **when Jesus argues with Pharisees about healing on the Sabbath**, he draws from that 2nd tradition, **the liberation tradition**—saying:
"What better day is there than the Sabbath for making straight the crooked path,
lightening the load of the heavy burdened,
and liberating the lives of the loveless and luckless."

And as we read today, when push comes to shove, he shoves the severe restrictions of **Sabbath rest** out of the way for the sake of that tradition of **Sabbath liberation**, declaring "The sabbath was made for humankind, and not humankind for the sabbath; so the Son of Man is lord even of the Sabbath."

And with all that background in place, the question again, "Why do people go to church on the Sabbath?"

In a sense we don't, Sabbath traditionally is from Friday at dusk to Saturday at dusk.
The majority of Christians, however, go to church on Sunday, in order to worship on the day Jesus was raised from the dead.

But, there is a touch of Sabbath on Sunday in worship. We keep it, (and, just so you know, I'm now parroting Luther's explanation of how Sabbath and worship

go together...)
    We keep it, to break up the routine of work work work, or work play work play work play—so that we can find an opportunity to inject the Holy into these weekly cycles by participating in public worship. And this public worship we do, is holy because we **hear God's Holy Word** and we **praise God** through song and prayer.
    And of course, I'm preaching to the choir here, you all showed up, you honor the holiness of time by being here. **And I do want to say to you all by being here you are doing something good and holy.**

    Yet, in a sense, it is not enough to just show up—Luther points to a peasant, who over-indulged the night before, waking up in pig trough, cuddling with a sow, so hung over he couldn't make it to church to hear the Word of God—and says "and yet those who come to worship and neither learn nor retain the promises of Christ are no better off." They too have broken the Sabbath.

    Still, for Luther, Sabbath does retains a sense of rest as well. We keep Sabbath for the sake of **our bodily needs**—we carve out as a society a time when everyone has a chance to stop from slaving away at work, because without rest we grow weary, crazy, and less human.
    So, in addition to reflecting on God's good promises as found in scripture, Sunday ought to be a time that is "good... for nothing." Just good to be, and to rest, and to reside in the goodness of God's world.

    In short, Sabbath is about rest, liberation, and holiness.
    It's about rest, a time that is "good... for nothing."
    It is also about liberation, acts of kindness and

justice are part of living into the holiness of God's time.

It, finally, is holy in and of itself, dragging us into the reality of God through our worship together in which we receive and cherish the promises of God.

A+A.

4. Gay Marriage
(Genesis 2:18-25, Leviticus 20:13, and Romans 1:24-2:5)

Today, we continue the summer sermon series, <u>20 questions in 10 weeks</u>, with two questions about Gay Marriage.
They are, **"Should we be sponsoring same sex marriage?"**
And **"Does the Bible profess marriage as between a man and a woman?"**

I'm kinda glad this question came up, as one of the decisions at Synod Assembly was that, in light of New Jersey allowing marriages between people of the same gender, every congregation should re-examine our 2009 statement on Sexuality <u>"Human Sexuality: Gift and Trust."</u>

Now, by way of beginning it's important to point out that part of the ELCA's statement "Human Sexuality: Gift and Trust" involved the concept of Respect for the Bound Conscience of the Neighbor
—the idea that brothers and sisters in Christ can deeply disagree with one another and still recognize the other person comes to their position from a place of faith.

Within our tradition it is acceptable to fall **anywhere** between the two following positions:

1. It's acceptable, to believe that same-gender sexual behavior is sinful, contrary to biblical teaching, and natural law. That same-gender sexual behavior carries the grave danger of unrepentant sin,
<u>and therefore</u> it is safe to conclude that the neighbor, and the community, are best served by calling people in same-

gender sexual relationships to repentance for that behavior and to a celibate lifestyle. **Such decisions are intended to be accompanied by pastoral response and community support.**

2. It's also acceptable, to believe that the scriptural witness does not address the context of sexual orientation and committed relationships that we experience today. That the neighbor and community are best served when same-gender relationships are lived out with lifelong and monogamous commitments that are held to the same rigorous standards, sexual ethics, and status, as hetero-sexual marriage
<u>And Therefore,</u> it is imperative to surround such couples and their lifelong commitments with prayer, that they might live in ways that glorify God, find strength for the challenges that will be faced, in order to serve others. Same-gender couples should avail themselves of social and legal support for themselves, their children, and other dependents and seek the highest legal accountability available for their relationships in their respective state"... **in New Jersey that means Marriage.**

So, to reiterate, both those extremes, and everything in the middle, are acceptable and faithful ways for members of the ELCA to understand Homosexuality and relate to gay-folk.

For the sake of full disclosure I fall **decidedly** in the 2nd camp. I am convinced by scripture, and witnessing the spiritual fruits of such relationships,
that same-gendered couples should be afforded every protection under the law,
and bear every responsibility of the faith,

with regards to their publically accountable, lifelong, monogamous, relationship.
They should get married and do so amongst God's people.
For me to profess anything other than that, would go against conscious.
Let us pray

    To answer the question: "Does the Bible Profess marriage as between a man and a woman?" the best place to start is in the beginning, or at least within spitting distance of it.
    The starting place for thinking about marriage, and in a lot of ways the starting point for natural law arguments against gay marriage too, is this beautiful and tragic account of man being without a partner.
    The man experienced the fullness of creation and says, "(Sigh) I need a partner, a help-mate, a wife."
    And God said, "It isn't good for Man to be alone."
    And God trots out companion after companion before him
—does a barn cat fill that hole in your heart? A dog, they're man's best friend, right? A hippo? Birds and bees?
    No, "for the man there was not found a helper as his partner."
    And so God took drastic measures, instead of digging deep again into the *hummus* to form a *human* partner, God digs into the man himself, and fashions from the very flesh of man a companion. God forms an Ishah from an Ish—a Wo-Man from a Man.
    And the man looks upon this companion and says:
'This at last is bone of my bones
  and flesh of my flesh.'

This second chapter of Genesis asks the question "Why is it, couples leave their flesh and blood, their family, and become a new family? Why does marriage and sex make you feel so very connected to the other person? Why is there such a tight bond between husband and wife?"

And the answer is because they too become flesh and blood. /In marriage, they become one flesh.

Why do most people yearn for "their other half?" Why do they so strongly seek a mate? Because it's natural! That yearning is innate within us!

So that's where marriage being between a man and a woman comes from
—from this explanation of the creation of new families,
this explanation of the fullness found in finding your other half,
your flesh and blood,
your rib so long removed from you,
finally returned.

There are also found in scripture five verses which prohibit sex between people of the same gender.

Several are found amongst the purity laws, for example in Leviticus 20 "And if a man lie with mankind, as with womankind, both of them have committed abomination: they shall surely be put to death; their blood shall be upon them."

Of course, as we read last week, if we go down this road, we'll need to round up everyone who worked on the Sabbath and kill them.

If we follow the admonition to kill all children who have ever talked back to their parents, we're not going to have much of a youth group left.

For that matter, (Bob, Randy, Eric)—following

Leviticus 14, I've inspected the education wing on more than one occasion, and have reason to believe there is at least some mold there, therefore we need to go out to the Mighty Fortress and get all our gasoline and pour it on the education wing, light it on fire, raze it to the ground, and take whatever is left to the local place of impurity.

In short, straight people applying purity laws only when they don't apply to us, is unfaithful.

The best place to go for prohibitions against same gender sex would be Paul, he's at least consistent. He's against all marriage, advising all Christians to stay celibate like he is, but if they're too weak for that, to get married—though he warns getting married leads to much distress.

Paul advises this, on one hand because he thinks the world is ending sooner rather than later,
but also because he believes marriage and sex can not be divorced from a Roman understanding of Power, which insists on separating people out into categories like Slave and Free, Citizen and Barbarian, Gentile and Jew, Male and Female
—in order to ensure one of those two categories **is in charge and powerful**, and the other is **disempowered, disenfranchised, and victimized.**

In fact, one of the main places people turn to, in order to dismiss gay marriage, Romans chapter 1, which we just read, is one of those places where Paul is kicking these lines of **division** in the teeth in the name of Jesus Christ.

Paul is writing to a divided community in Rome. A community filled with both Jewish and Gentile Christians, in which the Jews had been expelled from Rome for 5 years and then returned.

Imagine half of St. Stephen, let's say all but one council member and everyone who sits on the pulpit side, being removed from New Jersey by the government, and then coming back in five years time. Things would be different, you might even resent those who replaced you on council or who are sitting in "your" pew.

Well, Paul writes to this community, and is insisting that everyone, both Jew and Gentile, is a sinner in need of Christ's love.

So Paul sets a Rhetorical **trap**,
he **ensnares** his reader with his words.
He makes his argument by paraphrasing a Jewish book which talks about how sinful gentiles are, <u>The Wisdom of Solomon.</u>

Imagine this being read aloud to the whole community:
"Hey, fellow Jews" the letter begins *"remember what you've read in <u>The Wisdom of Solomon</u> about those sinful Gentiles who've taken over your church?*
*They're so horrible that they worship the **creature** instead of the **Creator**, and therefore the **Creator** allows them to fall into degraded and impure lust—instead of loving the **Creator** they lust for the **creation**.*
--At this point those Jewish Christians begin to nod in agreement. (They've read Wisdom of Solomon before, they know where this is going)
Once those gentiles head down the slippery slope of Idolatry
—and we know they do because they're Gentiles after all—
they'll continue falling further from God and the natural order of things, they'll be disordered, and will have unnatural sex with members of the same sex because Lust

is the only thing left in their hearts—those Gentile Sinners.
-- The Gentile Christians start to grumble, the Jewish Christians smile ear to ear.
And from there it just gets worse, doesn't it? All wickedness will pour out—Evil, coveting, malice, envy, murder, strife, deceit, craftiness, gossip, slander, hatred of God, disrespect, arrogance, foolishness, faithlessness, heartlessness, ruthlessness.
Those Gentiles are so bad they deserve to <u>die</u>!
-- One of the Jewish Christians might even shout out an Amen at this point.
"*And therefore,*" the reader continues, "*my fellow Jewish Christians **you have no excuse**, by judging others, <u>you are guilty</u>. **You Do The Same Thing!**"*

It's just like when Nathan tells David the story about the horrible man who stole a sheep, and David says "That man should die." And then Nathan responds, "You are that man."

Or, it's like a friend of mine who looked at the ELCA's statement on Human Sexuality to read about the sins of gay people, only to find that in its 44 pages there were only 2 pages about gay-folk, the rest was about straight folk and our sexual inclinations.
The point of this verse is that all, both Jew and Gentile, are in need of Christ.
Now I'm not saying Jesus or Paul were high fiving homosexuals in the 1st century
—instead I'm saying there was no such thing as homosexuality in the 1st century...
there was **only homoeroticism—only same-sex-acts**.
Roman Males had sex with Slaves and Women, Greek Males had sex with Boys and Woman.

Sex was used to affirm power and create those categories that Paul is so **insistent** are **inconsistent** with the Christian faith.
Marriage and sexuality both gay and straight, expressing love, commitment, and trust, just wasn't the norm back then, but it is now.

So that answers the first question, what's the Bible have to say about marriage being between a man and a woman, as well as the implied question of what does it have to say about same-sex-marriage.

As for the 2nd question, **"Should we be sponsoring same sex marriage?"**
Lutherans have a different relationship to the state than most denominations—it goes all the way back to Luther being protected by the princes while thinking through his faith—
The logic, I think, goes **"Wow, the fanatical religious folk want to assassinate me, the secular state is keeping them from doing so... maybe there is a place in my faith for a division between the Kingdom of Heaven and the Kingdom of Government!"**
Marriage isn't a sacrament.
The church blesses what the state has done, that why a traditional European Lutheran wedding often involve the long parade from the court house to the church.

Additionally, marriage isn't **just** about sex.
To quote the ELCA's sexuality statement, "Christians believe that marriage is not solely to legitimate physical sexual intimacy, but to support long-term and durable communion for the good of others."

I think of two gay seminary class mates, married in Massachusetts—a more traditional Lutheran couple you will not find, an organist and a Pastor—when they look at one another you *know* it's not *just* about sex, it's about love and commitment.

I think of one of my professors, raising her son along with her wife. Their marriage supports their parenting, it's a safe place from which to raise him.

I also think of *when* my good friend and colleague Pastor Fred and I get to grumbling:
Like Adam I say, "(Sigh) Being a Pastor is so hard and emotionally draining, I can't do it alone, I need a partner, a help-mate, a wife."
And Pastor Fred responds, like Adam, "(Sigh) Being a Pastor is so taxing, I can't do it alone, I need a partner, a help-mate, a husband."
Having sex doesn't lighten the load of being a Pastor, having someone to come home to, who you trust and love, who is flesh of your flesh and bone of your bone, **that does.**

In summary:
There is a wide variety of ways to understand marriage and be a faithful member of the ELCA.
Any pointing to purity laws to justify discrimination or worse against gay folk, if followed through logically, would have such severe consequences for **everyone in our society**, it could make the Salem witch trials, reign of the Taliban, or ISIS, or Boko Haram look tame.
We are truly at a different place than people in the 1st century were—Romantic love, especially between same

gendered individuals, just wasn't a thing, but it is now.

I'm wholeheartedly convinced marrying gay folk is not baptizing gay sex, but instead creating a healthy and holy space for legitimate yearnings for companionship, the protection of gay parents, and the strengthening of the institution of marriage. A+A

5. The Law and Christian Life
(Galatians 2:7-10 and Acts 15:19-21)

As we continue on our summer sermon series, 20 questions in 10 weeks, today's question is a pretty big one that I think will help us think about some of the previous questions we've tackled that are directly linked to laws found in the Old Testament, specifically the questions about Same Gender Marriage and Sabbath.
Today's question is, "Which Old Testament Laws do Christians have to follow?"

Before I get into the thick of things I think it is worth recommending everyone go home and read Luther's explanation of the 10 commandments as found in his Small Catechism, because that's not the direction I'm going today.

This question about Old Testament laws is one that was first dealt with by the early church at the Jerusalem Council, the record of which we find in both the *15th chapter of the Acts of the Apostles*, as well as in the *2nd chapter of Paul's letter to the Galatians*.
Let us pray

Both Acts and Galatians agree on why the first council of Jerusalem was called. It was about the question of circumcision.
Paul and Barnabas were serving a Gentile church in Antioch, Syria and came into conflict with Jewish Christians from Jerusalem who insisted they were preaching a false gospel, because these Jewish Christians believed to become Christian you need to become Jewish first. More

specifically, they needed to accept the most physical of community boundary markers—circumcision.

If you've ever read anything by Paul, you'll know very clearly his response to such requirements. **Not only no, but hell no**.

So Paul goes before the Apostles and they discuss his Christian mission to reach the gentile world, and come up with simple guidelines for Gentile Christians to follow—essentially they ask "Which Old Testament Laws do **Gentile** Christians have to follow?"

And that's where Paul and the author of Acts, we'll call him Luke, disagree.

Luke says the decision made at the Jerusalem Council was that Gentiles needed to follow four Old Testament Laws:
They must refrain from eating food offered to idols, as it is written in Exodus 34,
Meat that has been strangled or containing blood, as in Leviticus 17 and 3.
And they must be sexually chaste, as in Leviticus 18.

These are all laws found in the Torah said to apply not only to Jews, but also to gentiles living with Jews.

So, as Luke understands the Council's decision, Gentile Christians are **only** to follow the Old Testament Laws which **were put in place for Gentiles**, and specifically put in place to *make sure non-Jews don't do offensive things in the presence of Jews.*

In other words, if Jewish and Gentile Christians are in community together the Gentile Christians need to make sure they don't do things which would break <u>fellowship</u> with their Jewish Christian brothers and sisters.

So that's Luke's account of what Paul and the Apostles decided. **It is not however, Paul's account of that decision.**

Paul's answer to the question, "Which Old Testament Laws do Gentile Christians have to follow?" is much simpler. It is "Remember the poor." That's it...

Okay, maybe that's not **it**. The phrase "Remember the poor," is actually rather complex once you start looking at the other places where Paul speaks in similar terms.

At face value of course this is an admonition to take care of the least of these,
 to not turn away from the poisonous effects of poverty, or forget that we are all beggars.
All themes we can find throughout the Old Testament and especially in the Prophets.

But, for Paul, the Poor doesn't **just** mean the actual poor, but also **the Church in Jerusalem**, the **saintly apostles**.

In addition, to a basic economic understanding of "The Poor,"
he is also speaking of his ongoing **"collection for the poor among the saints in Jerusalem,"** as he calls it in his letter to the Romans.

He understands full fellowship between Jewish and Gentile Christians as involving **money**,
that the ethnic divisions of his time were most plainly bridged by economic interdependence,
a sharing of funds for the sake of the ministry.

Few things connect you to another person, like co-signing their lease/
 Few things get your skin in the game, like green-backs

riding on that game.

Yet, even that doesn't fully get to where Paul is going with this collection. He sees the collection as a fulfillment of prophecy.

Remember, the reason the three gentile wise men show up bearing gifts for the Baby Jesus in Matthew, was to fulfill prophecies about the wealth of the gentiles flooding into Jerusalem...
so too, Paul believed the collection **from the gentile churches** was cut from the same clothe—it was an end-times act, it was a fulfillment of the scriptures.

So, again, to the question, "Which Old Testament Laws do Christians have to follow?" It would seem between Paul and Luke's interpretations of the 1st council of Jerusalem,
we end up with rules that try to bridge relationships between Christians who are different from one another.

The basic rules for us, **are rules that bind us one to another.** They bind us economically to one another, but they also bind us to a modicum of decency and consideration for the sensibilities of our brothers and sisters in Christ.

But, there is a bigger point to be made here. Faith is not about rules, but about trust in the one who meets us in Baptism.

Andrew James Forys, there are many laws that bind you, many rules by which you will be judged.
There are rules about sex and Sabbath, money and mold, religious scruples and regard for parents, and you will probably be **judged as wanting** in at least some of those

areas, but that doesn't separate you from the love of God in Christ Jesus our Lord.

The amazing thing about our Lord is that he acts for us, even before we know how to act.

Our Lord promises life,
even when we are in death,
Promises salvation,
even as we are oppressed by Sin.

Jesus, through the water and the word, make us his siblings, binds us to the family of God our Father, through the power of the Holy Spirit.
A+A

6. Reward, Equality, Baptism
(Galatians 3:27-28 and Matthew 5:17-20)

As we near the end of our summer sermon series, 20 questions in 10 weeks, today's questions are about Reward, Equality, and Baptism.

Todays question is: **"Reward" in heaven is mentioned many times in scripture. Yet, it is not what we do, but what Christ does, that saves us. What does "greatest" and "least" in the Kingdom of Heaven mean? How does that square with "neither Greek nor Jew" etc,? Aren't we all equal?"**

Yipes.
Let us pray.

I must begin by stating that I set up this sermon series with the easier questions, one's I'd already reflected upon in one way or another and felt confident in answering at the start, which was great... until... we're no longer at the start.

Reward—a word that causes Lutherans everywhere to sneer, or at least one that only crosses our lips with great trepidation
—after all, reward suggests there is something to reward
—specifically a work, an action, that we can just do something.
Reward has the danger of nullifying grace, making God's works into a mock movement of man.

Yet, as the question says, reward language pops up frequently, it flows freely from Jesus' lips—proof that Jesus wasn't a Lutheran, I guess.

And it's not like Lutherans don't know this, that we don't read our Bible, or something like that, we've struggled with reward language since Luther nailed his 95 thesis to the wall.

According to Article 4 of the Apology of the Augsburg Confession, one of the documents we as Lutherans affirm to be a right interpretation of scripture, there are several things that can be said about reward.

1. At our most bold "we concede that works are truly meritorious" and can receive a reward, but **not** "the forgiveness of sins or justification." As a rule, when we hear reward language we recognize that such rewards only come in light of being made right by Jesus, that faith is implied whenever there is any talk of fruits of good works.

Essentially, the indignities suffered because of living our Christian faith, led by the Spirit, will find a parallel reward. If the Islamic State chops off your head like John the Baptist, your head will be held high in Heaven—that kind of thing.

Honestly, as North American Christians, I fear very few of us will have to worry about such rewards.

2. Additionally, when we read of rewards, we ought to remember Augustine's maxim, "God crowns his own gifts in us." That is, eternal life can be called a reward because it is owed to the Justified on account of a promise, that promise being the unconditional one made to us in Jesus Christ.

3. When talking of heavenly reward the question you ought to ask yourself is "does such talk assuage your conscience?"

We know the promise that God is merciful and passes over, and frees us from, our trespasses, faults, sins, and mistakes, brings us peace. We don't know if talk of reward does the same, in fact, from experience, we know it does not. At our death bed we want to hear about the loving actions of God for us, not about our own actions.

So, when we read about rewards in heaven we are not talking about our salvation, or if we are, we're talking about God rewarding us because of the promise found in Jesus Christ, and finally, the reason reward makes us feel squirmy, is that at face value it could make us trust in our own goodness, which often is lacking.

As for Jesus' talk about the least and the greatest in heaven, it is preached in the same breath as the beatitudes "blessed are the poor, the hungry, and the weeping."
It is part of Jesus' inversion of values, Jesus taking the God's eye view, instead of the human view.
Proclaiming that when God rules, the last are first and the first are last.
That as people of God it is important to look at the world through the cross, to look at our world and remember where we find Jesus—outside the city walls, among oppressed, suffering with them, killed with them.
This is very similar to that first way of talking about rewards in heaven—on earth you are tear gassed, depressed, and besieged, but in heaven you are enthroned, joyous, and protected. The God's eye view of the world is so very different. Those who appear least are greatest and greatest least.

Finally, how does this square with Paul's baptismal affirmation that in Christ there is no longer Jew or Greek, slave or free, male or female?
In Baptism we are entering into that God's eye view, we're struggling—just as the Galatians and Paul himself struggled—to live into who we are together
—live into our calling to be part of the Body of Christ

—live into the vision of humanity set out by God through Jesus Christ.

A vision that breaks down barriers between believers and allows for nothing to get in the way of life together resting in God's grace.

And Taylor, today,
Today you will enter into this vision.
Today you will become a part of the body of Christ.
Today that promise of God will be made concretely to you in the waters of Baptism.
Today you will be baptized with Christ Jesus. Baptized into his death and raised to a brand new life—united with Christ.
A+A

7. Suffering and Death
(1 Corinthians 15:25-26 and Colossians 1:24-2:5)

In this, our 2nd to the last sermon in the series "20 Questions in 10 Weeks" today's questions are about a Pauline view of suffering and death.
More specifically the two questions are,
1. "Colossians 1:24 states, "Completing what is lacking in Christ's afflictions" question mark.
2. Explain, "Death has died."
While that second phrase is not explicitly found in scripture, I assume it to be a riff on Paul's message in 1 Corinthians 15 and in Romans 6.
Both questions are about the meaning of scripture associated with the Apostle Paul. Therefore, today I'm going to try and do a little Paul to you all, in the hopes that it will answer these two questions.
Let us pray.

So, what does it mean to complete what is lacking in Christ's afflictions? What does it mean that Death has died?
My short answer is this:
The Church Universal, in this in-between time, suffers while fulfilling the Great Commission, so that Christ may be all in all.
Let me break that down for you.

The Church Universal:
A **community** that transcends all borders both of space and time, which is created in **Baptism** and is a part of the life, death, and resurrection of Jesus Christ.
In this in-between time:
We live in the already/not yet. Christ has already completed the redemption of the world, but it is not yet so.

We **have been** buried with Christ and we **are** suffering with him and we **will** be raised with him.

The world itself is in **labor**, the new creation will be **born**, yet we are in the labor **pains**.

We were wounded, and we will be healed, but right now that wound itches so very much.

Normandy was stormed on D-Day, but it isn't VE-Day yet.

We are at an in-between time.

Suffers:

This is the crux of it, I guess.

The Colossians are a Gentile group of Christians—that is non-Jews, presumably formerly Pagan. They were led astray, they decided to **add** on to their Christian faith. They added worship of angels and astrological adoration. Additionally, and more to the point, they likely practiced a severe form of asceticism—**ritual suffering in order to have visions.**

To this Paul responds, "You don't need to whip yourself or starve yourself to be a good Christian, if you try to *consistently* live in **faith, hope, and love**, you will surely have struggle enough without adding to it."

As for Paul, he knew plenty about suffering.

He experienced the suffering that comes with **conversion**, losing his former life and religious certainties that day when he fell from his horse on the Road to Damascus.

Suffering imprisonment, beatings, stoning, shipwreck, that famous and unnamed "thorn in his side" and all the dangers of the constant travel that accompanied his proclamation of the Gospel.

Suffering the experience of planting community after community, but never **staying** there long enough to see through his vision—only able to hear of the controversies in his young communities and respond in letter form, suffering as well the sadness that comes with not completing his most cherished wish, to form a Christian community in Spain.

While fulfilling the Great Commission:

This suffering is suffering for a purpose, it is completing Christ's body, by **spreading the Gospel**, or borrowing Paul's language—"Making the word of God fully known" **and making new Christians**, through the act of Baptism.

It is also completing Christ's body, by sustaining and building up the Christian Community—"presenting everyone mature in Christ," making sure we are following after Jesus, making sure we're disciples.

Or to put all that another way, when we follow the Great Commission found at the end of Matthew's Gospel, "Go therefore and make disciples of all nations baptizing them in the name of the Father, the Son, and the Holy Spirit," it will take **effort** and **time** and **treasure** and yes **suffering**, but it is a suffering **for the sake** of the Body of Christ, **completing** that body of Christ.

So that Christ may be all in all:

That the whole creation will find redemption.

That all of us will find ourselves in the fullness of the Body of Christ.

That even that last enemy, **death**, will be destroyed.

That through the Life, Death, and Resurrection of Christ, we can truly say Death has died.

The Church Universal, in this in-between time, suffers while fulfilling the Great Commission, so that Christ may be all in all. A+A

8. Sin and Forgiveness
(Romans 6:15-23 and Matthew 16:13-19, 18:15-18)

On this, our final sermon in the 10 week sermon series "20 questions in 10 weeks" our final group of questions are about Sin and Forgiveness.
They are:
1. Are mistakes "sins"? Are there degrees of sins? Is the sin in the intent or in the action or in the consequences? Ie. If you intend to do something good for someone and it turns out to hurt them?
2. Explain "Keys to the Kingdom." "Which you bind on earth shall be bound in heaven" etc.

A very short answer to these questions would be
1. They are all Sin and effects of Sin.
2. For Lutherans the key to "the Keys of the Kingdom" is the Word of God comforting our consciences.
Let us pray.

One of the biggest misunderstandings about the faith is the way most people think of Sin.
We assume it involves discrete acts, <u>s</u>in<u>s</u>.
Just from a visual perspective, we mess around with S's when we think through Sin. We make the first S lowercase, when it should be upper-case, and we add a second s, making it plural.
We go from Sin with a big S to sins with two small s's.

We worry about individual acts, things we can control. And in doing so, we shrivel up the Gospel and the Church, making the first a **rule book** and the second a

social club or **museum**.

Little sins can't explain the bizarre brokenness of the world we live in.
Maybe it can explain the shooting of Archduke Franz Ferdinand that started World War One, but it can't explain the mechanized destruction that followed that shot.
Maybe it can explain an affair, but not all the broken pieces that led to that betrayal or the consequences thereafter.
Maybe it can explain a child left to starve, but not the situations that led to such wretched poverty.

We recognize that Sin is so much bigger than individual peccadilloes or immoderation or wrong action. We recognize that Sin permeates everything.
It's as if, each and every last one of us, is a card within a house of cards. We were all, theoretically, stacked carefully and precariously atop one another. Even the slightest breath, a slight jarring of the table, would cause the whole house to fall down.
And that deck of cards is fallen, and we are constantly struggling fruitlessly toward our proper placement.
Every mistake is a card falling,
every intent, action, and consequence,
every one of the sins plural with a small s,
are cards knocking down the whole deck.
This deck is in a constant flurry of motion, Jacks falling atop crazy eights, and twos upon Kings. Every time a wall of a house is reconstructed two more fall down. The interactions of these cards grow in intensity until they become a splashing, bubbling, sea of black, red, and white.

Sin with a capital S is, to quote Paul, **slavery**. Human beings have sold ourselves, or perhaps been captured, by Sin and made to be its slave.

Or to borrow another image, we're addicts, we're addicted to Sin and cannot free ourselves.
Even *if* we were able to resist our addiction on our own, we'd still be a dry drunk—acting out as if drunk, while still sober—going along sinful pathways and experiencing the effects of Sin—even if we didn't commit sins plural-lower-case.

And so I proclaim this to you sisters and brothers, the good news of Jesus Christ's actions for us, are not that he patched up our hang-nail.
Not that he knows you fudged your taxes and looked the other way.
Not that he forgives you of your plural-little-s sins.

The Gospel is that Jesus has contended with a maelstrom of Sin, and he has calmed the storm, he has stood atop Sin's back in triumph, he has defeated it.
That Jesus has **bought** us out of slavery because he's our brother and that's what brothers do for their siblings. That Jesus has stormed the slave house, snapped our chains, and smuggled us out of Sin's grasp.
That Jesus brings us through the detox which comes with addiction—as the Good Physician. That he stands out in the parking lot as we chain smoke with a bunch of other sinners struggling together, that Jesus travels with us the whole way, even though we are always in recovery, even though we "remain sinners to the grave."

Yes, Jesus is freeing us from Sin with a capital S.

And it's worth proclaiming this loudly and often, because that's really what the Power of the Keys is about.

It's about speaking the gospel to people who have terrified consciences,
who see the swollen effects of Sin upon their lives and feel hopeless,
who need a word of grace in the midst of their guilt and loss and sorrow and struggle.

And this isn't just something for the Pastor to do alone. It's what we all ought to do.

Every day we hear confessions small and large—not in a formal way you understand—but naturally,
A conversation between neighbors,
a son's words of worry to his father,
a coffee mate's confession.

And to all these we can speak a word of truth about God being for us, not against us.
In all these we can be a beggar telling another beggar where we got some bread.

In the midst of dealing with the effects of Sin, both small and large, it is so important for people to know that Sin, with a big S, with its death dealing ways, has been defeated by the free gift of God, eternal life in Christ Jesus our Lord.

A+A.

Year 2

9. The Trinity
(Luke 1:30-35, 3:21-22 and John 1:1-5, 20:21-23)

Grace and Peace to you, on this Trinity Sunday.
And not only that, but Grace and Peace to you on this first Sunday of our 8-week sermon series in which questions from the pews are answered in the pulpit.
Today's question is exceedingly relevant to this day in the church year, Trinity Sunday.
The question is this: *"In the Apostles Creed it says Jesus was conceived by the Holy Spirit. In the Nicene Creed it says that the Holy Spirit proceeds from the Father AND THE SON. What gives?"*
So essentially, the question becomes, "Jesus comes from the Holy Spirit and the Holy Spirit comes from Jesus, how does that work?"

The first thing we need to consider is that we can talk about the Trinity in multiple ways.
On one hand we can talk about the inner Being of God.
On the other hand we can talk about our experience of God, about how God has interacted with God's people from the beginning.
An imperfect analogy for these two ways of thinking about the Trinity would be the difference between being part of a Family
versus
looking at a family from the outside.
Think about the things you can say about your own family dynamics that you really can't say about those of your neighbor's family, no matter how much you know about

them.
　　Simply put, from the outside you can only understand so much. **Inner Being and Outward Experience are two very different things.** This is true of both family life and the Trinity.
　　Yet, in this sermon I'll try to talk a bit about the Being of God as expressed in the Creeds, and then about the Experience of God for all of us.
Let us pray

　　To begin, it is worth noting most Heresies are caused by **saying too much**—about nailing things down too fully (putting God in a box).
Orthodoxy—*saying something right about God*, on the other hand, is so often taking the middle ground between two extremes. And so it is with the Trinity.
　　The faith, as found in the creeds, threads the needle between two extremes—Modalism and Arianism.
　　Modalism was a view of the Trinity that simply said, "1 God is 3 because that one God comes to us in three ways." (The Ice/Water/Steam analogy) In Modalism it's as if God put on three different masks—different modes of being. So Modalism's focus is on the oneness of God **above all other concerns.**
　　As you can imagine this wreaks havoc on what scripture says about God. Think of Gethsemane, "Father take this cup from me." **It's like Father and Son are a ventriloquist act.**
　　The response to Modalism in the **West** was to define God as one in Substance, Essence, and Nature, but three in Person. In the East they defined God as one in Will, but separate in Hierarchy—The Son and Spirit are subordinate to the Father.

This Eastern response to Modalism is where we get Arianism.

Arianism is an extreme form of this concern over the Hierarchy within the Trinity... eventually the question arises "How subordinate are Spirit and Son to the Father?" (Where do they fit in the pecking order?)
Are they in fact God, or just exalted creatures?
Are they God at all?
Is Jesus just a good man and the Spirit just the effects of God's actions?

Through a few quirks in history the Arian movement moves from the East to West and takes off in Northern Europe. Specifically these Arians deny the full Divinity of Jesus.
To combat this belief, the Western Church, around the 6th century, adds a line to the Nicene Creed, "The Holy Spirit Proceeds from the Father AND THE SON."

That's what's going on with these creeds—they are describing the Being of God in a way that doesn't go off the rails, either denying the **uniqueness** of Spirit and Son, or obliterating their **divinity**, claiming they are creatures.

But let's step back a bit, let's move from **being** to **experience**, from **Creeds** to **Scripture**.
<u>Let's get closer to an answer to the question!</u>

Firstly, there is a solid basis for this addition to the Nicene Creed—adding "And the Son."

As we read today Christ blows his Holy Spirit upon the Disciples—they receive the Spirit, which gives them peace and the power to forgive and retain sins.

Throughout John's Gospel the Holy Spirit is **so** connected to Jesus that it almost feels like it is a disembodied version of Jesus—Jesus' ghost if you will.

(Though it's worth nothing that in John, Jesus also calls the Spirit "Another Advocate.")

Still, the Apostle Paul talks about the Spirit as "The Spirit of Christ." And equates being filled with the Holy Spirit with having the "Mind of Christ."

Yes, the claim of Nicaea that, "The Spirit Proceeds from the Son," meshes with our experience as God's people as expressed in the New Testament.

At the same time, dear Mary points us to the other side of things. Her child, Jesus, is conceived by the Holy Spirit. His birth is the work of God, and we know that to be true because the Spirit, that "Shy Sovereign," has made it so, and seal his Sonship to God.

For that matter, at Jesus' Baptism the Spirit, like a dove, points to Jesus, declares, and affirms, that Jesus is the Son of God, the beloved of God.

Yes, the claim of Apostle's creed that, "Jesus was conceived by the Holy Spirit," stands in scripture.

Yet this mystery goes back far beyond these Gospels. Within the first three verses of Genesis we find Spirit and Word transforming the "Formless void."...

But to give some sort of answer, we might Spring boarding off the start of John's Gospel—we might say:

"The Pre-existent Son of God, the Word who was with God and was God, was brought into this world by the Power of the Spirit, and the Spirit affirmed Jesus' identity at his Baptism.

After Jesus' death and resurrection, and in a variety of ways, Jesus gave the Spirit to his disciples. The Spirit continues to point us to the mind-blowing reality that Jesus is God's Son.

And for that matter, in our Baptism, the Spirit, comes to us letting us know we are adopted into Jesus' family—we are made Children of God—connected to the Holy Mystery of the Being of God!

Through Son and Spirit we experience the Being of God. A+A!"

10. Sacrifice and Self Care
(Numbers 11:14-17 and Luke 10:25-37)

The question asked in this our 2nd of 8 question posed from the pews, is one that everyone struggles with to one degree or another—especially those who have a have a role as a caregiver—either officially or unofficial, in a paid capacity or an unpaid one.

Today's question is this: **"How do we balance our own happiness with the happiness of others?"**

Now I did talk with the person who put this question in the box—to get a clearer idea of what was meant.

And this question's author pointed out something really insightful
—when pastors **preach**, we frequently preach about self-sacrifice, about serving our neighbor in need, even if, maybe even especially when, that service is costly, when it's hard and risky.

At the same time, when the preacher acts **pastorally**, when we counsel or listen to a parishioner's problems, so frequently, we recommend self-care, we switch from **self-sacrifice** to **self-preservation**.

And this wasn't just me as Pastor, but every pastor the questioner had interacted with.

So, what's the balance? What's the faithful way to weight **self and other**?/ **sacrifice** and **self-care**?

The danger in this question
—is a common danger
—**it starts with an assumption of *scarcity*.**

It's as if there is only so much...

So much goodness, happiness, joy
Only so much to go around.
That either my cup is full and other people's cup is empty, or their cup is full and my cup is empty.
It's as if happiness is a commodity, to be bought and sold with our time and effort and even money.
Down that line of reasoning lies a place where happiness is horded—saved in little boxes to be savored alone...
But that's not the nature of happiness.

Happiness isn't water to fill a glass with, but an ocean to swim in, as our cup overflows.

Happiness isn't an item to be bought or sold, but a gift that is shared.

Happiness is like a Popsicle, if you try to horde it or hide it, it melts in your pocket and is gone.

Yes, Happiness is an overflowing thing—it grows when it is shared and shrinks when concealed and hidden away.

Yet the question remains, **"how do we find balance in life, so that we can be in relationship with other people in such a way that the joyful goodness of life may be shared?"**

I would suggest –the place to look is at the Lawyer's question in today's Gospel: "What must I do to inherit eternal life?"

The question that Jesus downgrades to simply, "Do this and you will live."

The equilibrium between our happiness and that of others, is balanced upon **not missing chances to be merciful**.

Self-sacrifice and self-care are balanced upon **opportunities to be merciful.**

Let us pray.

There was a woman going from Jerusalem to Jericho, and she was robbed, stripped of all she had, beaten, and left half dead.

Then along came a Priest, just by the thick trudge of her footfalls you could tell she was heavy laden
—she was embittered,
she was burnt out.
--you might say in modern parlance, she had caretakers fatigue.
--or going the other direction, looking backward, you might say she was a Moses figure.
Now, on at least two separate occasions in Hebrew Scripture this story of Moses giving up, and then learning to delegate, is told... *Perhaps it's important...*

Well, this Priest, she didn't take that story to heart. There she was, the walking dead—like Moses saying, "Kill me now."
So bedeviled by duty that when she looked at that dying woman, she thought, "Another obligation," and kept right on moving.
Perhaps she'd bought her own hype—that she alone could bring home the bacon... well she's a Jewish woman... so maybe she brought home the goods... maybe she believed that she alone could serve fully and serve well.
Perhaps she simply **couldn't say no** and this moment was the one chance she had, with no one looking over her shoulder, so he passed by.
So she grit her teeth and kept on keeping on, doing the things she was **obliged** to do, but not stooping down to do what she **ought** to do.

She missed a chance to be merciful because she tried to do it all by herself.

Then along came a Levite. Her steps were disordered, her movement erratic. She was watching a Youtube Video on her Smartphone in one hand, while also combing her hair with the other, as she slashed from one side of the street to the other.
In fact, she was so distracted that she tripped over the dying woman.
It didn't even phase her, she was overscheduled as it was—like Martha she was busy with many things—every moment scheduled... even her unscheduled moments were scheduled—no moment of serendipity allowed.
Like so many of her day she wore her busyness as a badge of honor.
But also, she kept busy, because when she didn't, when the multi-media extravaganza of modern life, the hypnosis of hypersecheduling broken, when it all stopped blaring, when there were quiet moments, she just didn't know what to do, how to be a person unscheduled and alone—free!
She missed her chance to be merciful because she was distracted.

There was a Samaritan too, who traveled on that long winding road from Jericho to Jerusalem.
She walked with a little skip in her step—she had a secret inside her she was willing to share.
She was loved—and she knew it.
She considered that famous phrase of Torah that Samaritans share with the Jews, "Love your neighbor... **as yourself."**
She recognized that life is a little like an airplane

ride—in case of emergency an oxygen mask may appear, in which case you need to secure your own mask before helping others.

So, she didn't overschedule herself—she didn't buy the prevailing culture's assumption that busyness was next to godliness.
She gave herself time to be—little Sabbaths—so that she could be fully with other people in their times of need.
She also recognized she wasn't the sole force of good in the world
—that many hands make light work
—that the alternative to delegating responsibility tends to be **resentment**.
She even said **"no"** sometimes—***and didn't feel bad about it either!***

She knelt down and administered aid to the woman. She did what she could for her, but knew there were people better equipped than her to heal the woman's every ill. She took her to an innkeeper who knew about ointments and healing, and together they showed her mercy.
She did not miss her opportunity to be merciful.
Upon that moment, self-sacrifice and self-care, sit together.
A+A

11. Salt, Light, and Hands
(Mark 4:10-13, 21-25 and Matthew 5:13-15, 6:1-4)

Today's questioner tackles a tension they see in scripture—a tension between two commands of Christ.
The question is this: "Explain how one should not "hide your light under a basket" and yet not "let your left hand know what your right hand is doing."
As with many passages in scripture, there are contradictions—some real, some imagined.
And this shouldn't surprise us—the record of God's actions among God's people strewn over a dozen centuries and 3 continents is going to contain some tensions.
But, the questioner might be a little worried, because this seeming contradiction—between revealing light and hiding actions—comes from Jesus' own lips... more than that, in one instance it comes from the same speech, **the Sermon on the Mount**, in the same Gospel, **Matthew's**!
So, in order to answer how we can **reveal light** and **hide hands**, we will have to answer a few prior questions.
"What light is supposed to be revealed?"
"What is Jesus getting at with these two commands?"
and finally,
"How do we do both?"

Prayer

1. The first thing to note is that Jesus' command to not "hide your light under a basket" is found in two gospels —the light not to be hid signifies different things depending on what gospel we are reading.

In the earliest of the two gospels, Mark
—Jesus is describing what a parable does to a person. It wraps up a truth, but the more we ponder the parable, the story, the more the truths encapsulated in the story come out.
A parable is like fuel to the fire of truth.
Soon enough the whole house is alight with it.
It's like I always say about Parables:
You are meant to chew on them, until they start to chew on you.

Matthew's Gospel, in contrast, places Jesus' admonition about not hiding your light under a basket within his Sermon on the Mount. He starts preaching immediately after healing those who come to him. After that healing, he blesses "poor, mourning, meek, hungry, peaceful, persecuted, people." Then he states, "You are the salt of the earth, you are the light of the world
—you can't be hid,
the lamp goes on the lamp stand and gives light **to the whole house."**
Think about that setting…
"You're healed now. You were poor, mournful, hungry, etc," now you're rich, joyful, and filled… don't misuse that gift, don't hide that fact. "Let your light shine before people, so that they can see your good deeds and give honor to your Father in heaven."

So, Mark's account is describing the fiery strangeness of Parables.
Matthew's Gospel describes the proper response to being healed
—the way in which grace
—the gift of God

—is a **calling** upon our life, it makes us to be people who point to our healing
 and work for the healing of others,
all to honor God.

2.	Let's go with this second use of do not "Hide your light under a basket," since it's the one found in the same speech as do not "Let your left hand know what your right hand is doing."

　　Sat next to one another, we quite quickly see the difference between the two—the point at which the seeming contradiction breaks down.
　　Shine forth your light **so they can give honor to God.**
　　Don't let your right hand know what your left hand is doing—give alms in secret—because otherwise you are "practicing your piety before others **in order to be seen.**"
　　See the difference? Pointing to God, or pointing to yourself.
-The first, is like the Olympic torch, it's lit by a previous torch and points backward toward an original one—that first Olympic game shrouded in mystery and myth.
-The second, is personal pyrotechnics—blowing something up so everyone turns their attention toward you for a moment.
It's Humility versus Hubris.
It's a question of **intention**
Jesus' point is that the inner purpose behind our actions shapes shape their meaning
—with our actions, do we intend to point to God our to ourselves?

3.	And that sounds good—but how can you tell the

difference? Sure, it's easy to interpret it *in other people*—humans are social animals and can usually sniff our hubris pretty well... but how about within ourselves?
How can we tell when we're lighting a torch instead of blowing something up?
How can we protect ourselves from hubris?
How can we make sure our intention is to point to God?

Through practice.
Think of the two examples of this light we have in Matthew and Mark's Gospels
—as a **parable** that burns you up inside and eventually appears on the outside pointing to a formerly hidden truth,
—and as **thanksgiving** to God for the blessed healing they've received through Christ Jesus.
That's part of the reason we all come to Church
—at least I hope it is...
we're practicing **stories so true that they burn us up inside**
and practicing **giving thanks for all that is from God.**

We do this for many reasons, but one of them is to work on our **intentions**. To transform our hypocrisies and hubris into **humility**.

How can we not practice our piety before others, yet shine forth our light in such a way that it honors God?
We change our intentions by :
Letting the strange and powerful stories of God shape us
And by seeing what God has given us and giving thanks.
A+A

12. Foreknowledge, predestination, and human will
(Exodus 9:8-12, 1 Samuel 6:1-9, and Matthew 13:10-17)

Today, is the 4th sermon in the sermon series, "8 Questions from the pews," we will tackle the question, "Matthew 13:10-15—Is this an example of pre-destination? It seems rather harsh and final, that whatever little they do have will be taken away."

My short answer is, "No. Matthew 13:10-15 is not about pre-destination. It's about why Jesus speaks in parables."

But that wouldn't be a very satisfying answer.

After all, there are larger questions lurking behind this question—questions about pre-destination and the harshness and finality of some of our sacred scripture.

To think about these questions we'll touch on the section of Matthew's Gospel we read today, but more concretely we'll consider Pharaoh's hardened heart.

So, we'll be looking at **pre-destination and the harshness of scripture.**
Prayer

When we consider pre-destination we tend to balk and then climb into one of two camps—the **puppet** camp or the **free will** camp.

In the first, we consider Pharaoh, and take the author of Exodus at his **most** literal. That the hardening of Pharaoh's heart, was a puppet show. God takes Pharaoh's heart, his will, and forces it in a certain direction.

You've heard the phrase, "Jesus take the wheel," this would be a little different, "Oh my, God has hijacked the vehicle!"

The LORD walks Pharaoh through a thought process and across a stage like a marionettist would his puppet.

If we go too far down this road we start to call everything fate. We become nothing more than debris on an ocean current. We lose a sense of agency and efficacy.

God becomes a character of Greek myth—the Fates. Three old Crones creating the lives of mortals on a mystical loom. As the thread thickens, so does our heart, when the thread snaps, our life is done.

At least, in this view of things, there is someone else to blame.

In the second camp, the free will folk, we turn into a young child, stamping our feet and always saying, **"I can do it my own self."**

We take the tact of the Philistines in the book of Samuel, and interpret Pharaoh's hard heartedness as something he has **chosen**.
We believe we have that power of choice.

We respond to John Donne's famous line, "no man is an island," with *"Na-ah, I'm an island!"*

We ignore any outside influence upon our lives. How our society shapes us, how our family forms us. We ignore that our self only exists in relationship with other people.

Ultimately, we ignore that we are "part of the main," because this radical *individuality* gives us a sense of power, and control in a fickle world.

But, as Lutherans, we affirm that our will is bound, "we are bound to sin and can not free ourselves."

We profess that we've sold out.

We say this often, but what does this mean? What does this look like?

We're saying that **of course** Pharaoh didn't relent. He couldn't,
   not because he was a puppet pulled around by the LORD, but because he was a **human being**.
   When confronted by a power greater than himself, something that threatened his narcissistic sense of control,
   He dived into himself.
   He defended his non-existent free will, shaped by forces he neither understood nor could control.
   The LORD hardened Pharaoh's heart simply by being **the Law** for Pharaoh there
—by giving limits to a man who considered himself god, by pointing out to him "you are mortal, I am God," Pharaoh's heart grew recalcitrant, because, **outside of the Gospel message**, this is almost inevitably the human response to being shown where we stack up in the universe
—seeing the world as it is, without also seeing God as God is, inevitably leads to a hardened heart.

   As for the question about harshness and finality, we can think of it this way: is this judgment on Pharaoh too harsh or too final? It is not.
   Pharaoh's heart is hard, *as are our own*. We just aren't often reminded of this fact.
   Likewise, is it hard to say, as it says in Matthew: "if you don't meditate on the parables of Jesus, the message will be lost on you/
but if you listen to his message it will blossom."

No, it is not too hard... because this is how Parables work, if you work on them, they work on you.
   As I say every chance I get, you chew on Parables

until Parables chew on you. You read them until they start to read you.

Is that harsh?

Yes, yet it's simply something like a law of the universe... a spiritual law sort of like physical laws... it is harsh only...

Only if gravity is harsh.
Only if Chemistry is harsh.
Only if cause and effect is harsh.

Yes, these things are harsh, and yes these things are final—immutable things.

But I thank God every day that Jesus' love steps beyond the harsh **cause/effect relationship** of our world.

I thank God that the way the world works, the way our hard hearts respond to an honest assessment of our place in the universe,
the way our unlistening ears ignore the best and deepest truths...

I thank God, that the final word is not by these things—the final word is His.

And it is not harsh, but instead a word of **comfort**, a word that plucks us out of our alternating throws of fatalism and false independence.

He takes our hearts of stone and makes them hearts of flesh.

He takes our ears and unstops them so that we might here the final word—the gentle comfort of the Word Made Flesh.

Thank you God, that in your greatness you free us from our bondage.

Thank you God, that in your greatness you unite us

to yourself and to one another as sister and brother.
Faced with this freedom and this fellowship, My heart... my soul...can not help but sing How Great thou art.

Let us sing together, How Great Thou Art.

13. Church Attendance
(1 Samuel 3:1-11, Psalm 137, Ezra 3:10-13, and Matthew 28:16-20)

Today's question, the 3rd in our sermon series "8 Questions from the Pews," is one the demographers have had their eye on pretty intensely for at least as long as I've been alive—though in these last few years the question has become more pressing.

The question is: "Why are there fewer people in Church? All over the place, not just here."

In the last quarter century the ELCA has shed a million and a half members.

So too the Episcopal Church... The UCC has plummeted from 2 million members at it's inception to under a million now... the Methodist church sheds 1,000 members a week and church attendance in the Roman Catholic Church has fallen from 77% in 1950 to 45% today.

In the last seven years 8% of Americans have stopped identifying as Christian and 7% more identify as non-religious.

So, it's not the questioner's imagination, in general we're shrinking.... And yes, "all over the place, not just here."

There are many reasons for it, but I'll talk a bit about three of them, the 3D's—
Disestablishment,
Decentralization,
and Demographics.

Pray

I like Samuel—not the man so much, but the idea, that he represents—where he sits *vis a vis* the history of God and God's people.

On one side of him is the period of God's history known for Bands of Prophets and Tribal Judges—for a loose league of tribes, a decentralized way of worshipping and leading.

On the other side of Samuel, is a period of time centered on a single monarch and a lone temple—a centralized structure of both religion and politics.

Yes, it is as God said, "See, I am about to do something in Israel that will make both ears of anyone who hears it tingle." Such change surely made the ears of many burn.

The Israel that existed before Samuel is unrecognizable to the Israel that exited after him. It was a mixed bag and a rough transition
—a time of civil war,
a time when the Levitical Priests outside of Jerusalem starved to death,
a time of prosperity and of unsettling change.

So too we are experiencing a sea change in **our** religious life.
We are experiencing the **Disestablishment** of the Church, the **Decentralization** of all things, and a shift of both ethnic and economic **demographics**.

1. We are experiencing **the Disestablishment of the Church**… there was a time when being a Good American Citizen and being a Good Christian were *seen* as the same. No more.

Now it's assumed Soccer Practice, or Pop Warner, or Reading the New York Times on Sunday Morning will make a good citizen just as well as Sunday School, Confirmation, or Church Attendance.

Fostering faith is no longer seen as a societal good. Social pressure will no longer regularly be put behind the Christian faith.

We are also experiencing extensive **decentralization**—that a small group of people without anyone in charge can now influence the world.
Think, as an example, of the two things that have shaped American life in the first decade of the 21st century— Terrorist and the Internet.

On 9/11 19 men dispersed among 4 groups, loosely connected, were able to kill nearly 3,000 people and radically change American domestic and foreign policy to this very day.

Or for that matter, think of the internet. A group of people, each working on their own for no pay, were able to create Wikipedia, a continually expanding online encyclopedia that dwarfs anything in print, and is available for free to anyone with an internet connection.

Compared to these things the Church can be a hulking unwieldy thing...

Decentralization fosters radical individuality and undercuts all centralizing authorities. All of a sudden every viewpoint is expressed, no matter how far out, and all of a sudden no viewpoint needs to be listened to. Everything becomes polarized and individualized.

Anything claiming to have, or be, a center, will not hold
—no authority has authority
—this includes:
the Church writ large,

Pastors,
and denominations.

    Finally, we are confronted by changing ethnic and economic **demographics** in America.

    One of the reasons people came to Church, especially Lutheran and Catholic Churches
—was to be with people who spoke the same language and came to America from the same country.
(we're sort of a victim of our own success) This is no longer something the average Lutheran seeks in a Church. For that matter, there are no new Lutherans coming from "The Old Country" to refill our pews.

    Additionally, the ELCA tends to draw members from the "middle class"—but in the last two—maybe the last four—decades what it means to be middle class—the demographic realities of that, have changed.

    There are few good manufacturing jobs, people are accruing massive student debt in order to get into the middle class, and there is a necessity of two incomes just to stay in the middle class.
It's squeezed the middle class and it's squeezed the Church.
The average person is now both time and money poor—so too the church.

2.   Now, like the Israelite Exiles in Babylon, we too feel lost. It can feel like this Demographically different, Decentralized nation that we have been Disestablished from, is a strange land. We may weep when we remember **the good old days**
—all change, even positive change, involves a loss
—it involves mourning.

But that's not the whole story
—there ought to be shouts of joy mixed with our earnest weeping. Like those returning from the Exile we can rightly weep when looking at the shrunken shroud of what once was a vibrant house of God.

At the same time, like them, we ought to shout for joy because the foundation of the House of the Lord is laid!

Yes, because of Disestablishment "The Game" might start before church finishes,
you can now buy things on Sunday,
Christianity won't regularly get a pat on the head from civic leaders, unless, you know, we actually do something special,
and at some point we'll probably have to start paying property tax on the Church and the Parsonage.

But that's not all bad.

Maybe being taxed will shock us into thinking about the difference between community and building, people and steeple.

Maybe the church will be freed from the shackles of **respectability**... because we no longer expect that pat on our head from society for upholding social niceties.

For example a clergyman more conservative than I, recently found out that Pub Theology meets in a bar, and he said to me, "Next thing you know you'll be talking to Prostitutes about Jesus won't you? What do your neighbor's think?" And I responded, "Isn't that what Jesus was accused of doing?" Shedding societal respectability to bring the Gospel to Sinners. "If I'm following Jesus why should I worry what the neighbors think?"

Yes, Decentralization undercuts our authority, denominational loyalty, and fosters radical individualism.

But maybe,
maybe this **decentralized, semi-anonymous, depersonalized internet age**
filled with crabby and hurtful people (*no really look at any comments section of any page on the internet*),
maybe this age could use the highly person community of the church as balm for its tired and hurting soul.
Maybe,
maybe Lutherans, the tradition that harnessed the Guttenberg press to spread the Word of God, can harness new technology for the same!
Maybe,
maybe the church is in fact a small group of people, who can influence the world,
and therefore **an era of decentralization is an exciting time to be Christian!**

Yes, Demographic shifts have us on the ropes, being a tradition tied to an ethnic identity no longer does us any favors, and being a middle class church just doesn't mean what it used to.
But maybe,
maybe we should consider that of the five countries with the most Lutherans in the world, two of them are African and one is Asian—and we need to get ready for the immigration of our sisters and brothers from Tanzania, Ethiopia, and Indonesia.
Maybe,
maybe this breaking of ethnic identity and religious identity will focus us on what makes us Lutheran
—because I swear to God, Lutheranism offers so much more than Lutfisk and blond braids or Bratwurst and Lederhosen
—ours is Grace,

ours is the Word of God,
ours is Cross.

For that matter, maybe the new economic reality we face will allow us to hear the cries of the poor more fully. Maybe this little **bite** of poverty we experience will point us to the **mauling** our brothers and sisters in poverty are experiencing.

3   In closing, ours is to be faithful, following after our Lord, Baptizing and making Disciples.
Doing so in whatever world we find ourselves.
Doing so whatever our relationship to wider society.
Doing so in large groups together or in small groups dispersed.
Doing so whatever our ethnic and economic composition.
     Yes—doing so, this very day.

Baptizing little Ryan into Christ right here today
—affirming that God is with him no matter what
—with him in this day of his Baptism,
with him in his old age,
in the morning of his life and noontime and evening.
With him,
with all of us,
as our life unfolds.

A+A

14. Religious violence
(Joshua 11:10-15, Psalm 23, Philippians 3:7-11, and Luke 22:47-51)

Today's, on this, our 6th sermon in the Summer Sermon Series "8 Questions from the Pews," I'll be tackling a topic that you might say is one of my hobby horses, maybe even a fixation: **the connection between religion and violence.**

It was on this subject, nearly 4 years ago, on the 10th anniversary of the attacks of 9/11, that I preached my first sermon as St. Stephen's pastor. Since then, at Pub Theology and in other sermons, I've covered similar ground.

In fact, judging by today's question, I may have, in these last 4 years, made my case too forcefully—that I've made a solid link between religion and violence in you all's mind.

The question is this:

"Religion is a source of hope and salvation for many, yet it has been the basis or cause of so many wars over time, why? And how do the positives negate all the negatives of war and radicals?"

To answer this questions we'll look at our text from Joshua in order to think about how violence can be connected to religion both in scripture and in history—then we'll consider why this connection get's made, and then finally I'll suggest a few ways these negatives can be upended or at least balanced.

Prayer

It would be foolish to ignore the connection between

religion and violence found in scripture.

Consider the fanatical acts described in **the book of Joshua**, utterly destroying towns and people in the name of Moses and the name of God. Truly this is disturbing stuff found in our scriptures.

And it's not the only place in scripture where we find dark acts dedicated to God.
We find rules about slavery and the oppression of women,
Calls to kill Babylonian and Assyrian Children,
Guidelines for war that are more concerned with trees than people,

And maybe there is a larger point that must to be made about these things:
Often scripture is being **descriptive** instead of **prescriptive**
—it's showing and telling, not ordering
—describing a lived reality, not making a program for life now.
It's faithful people at a particular time and place saying "wow, in the midst of it all God is here" so that we too might trust even in the most violent and strange of times, that God is here.

For that matter, it would be foolish to ignore the connection between religion and violence found in history.

Take for example a common interpretation and use of **the book of Joshua** from the 15th-17th century. When the *Conquistadores,* who took South America, read this biblical book—they did so in a **prescriptive** instead of **descriptive** way—they read themselves into the book
They justified their slaughter of natives and taking of land as a parallel to the taking of Canaan in the books of Joshua and Judges.

In fact, frequently colonization and invasion has been justified by faith—it is often said colonizers offer god, bring guns and germs, and leave with gold.

And there is that icky question left—once you get into it, why?

Why is religion linked to violence? Why does invasion and war often have a religious tint? Why is religion woven into matter of statecraft and splattered all over the history of war?

It could be that religion is innately violent, or that it encourages countries to colonize, or something like that, but I think not, instead, <u>religion speaks to our deepest selves</u> and about those things which are most important to us both individually and collectively. Everything else is of secondary importance—**imagine what kind of motivator our faith is!**

For example, an American drone kills your kid on the Afghanistan/Pakistan border—you want revenge... how much more of a motivation is it if you're told not only will you get revenge for your kid, but also God wants you to get that revenge!

What I'm saying is religion is often a **justification** for war and other acts of violence, not the actual **cause**.

Take, for example, the most "religious" of wars, the Crusades. The initial **Religious justification**—when Pope Urban the 2nd declared "*Deus Vult*" "God wills it" it was a call to defend Christians traveling to Jerusalem, and throughout the Middle East, from attacks by Muslims. Yet, somewhere along the line it became more profitable to pillage fellow Christians in Constantinople and throughout Asia Minor, so the **religious justification** for such actions shifted to fighting incorrect understandings of the trinity.

Two different acts of violence, both conveniently justified with a religious pretext.

So, what do we do with all that—how do we, to put it crassly, *"come out ahead?"* How can we be sure religion is *"worth it?"*

Well, firstly, it's important that we continue to wrestle with the ways in which our faith has fallen short—more than that, we ought to repent of it.

I think of former Presiding Bishop Mark Hansen's moving words about representing the ELCA as part of the Lutheran World Federation in Stuttgart Germany, where they confessed to and repented of our historical persecution of the Mennonite tradition—there our Mennonite sisters and brothers accepted our repentance and declared us forgiven.

And that right there—**receiving forgiveness**—for me that would be enough, that would upend all the negatives of being a religious people—that would, to quote the questioner be the positive that "negates all the negatives."

That this is a space where we can be honest about our faults and find forgiveness
—find a grace we don't deserve
—that alone is of infinite worth. As Paul writes all else is rubbish.

While it can be deeply misused, religion is the language of our deepest values. It frames our existence, cultivates holy habits, and tells stories that give life meaning.

Also it gives us comfort like nothing else will—just

think back to the last time you heard the 23rd Psalm, all that is packed into that, how those words travel with you through the very shadow of death.

Christ's words we read today "No more of this" ring so true, in the face of violence both scriptural and historical, **"No more of this."**

Faith is for healing the hurt, not hurting the healed. Yes, of course faith can be misused, but so can so many things
—If a child hits another child with a book, do we burn all books, or teach them to read?

The abuse of Religion, **bad religion**, can be best balanced by better religion.
And that's part of our calling—to put away swords and bring healing.
To do what Christianity has always been called to do, to recognize the good in those things that are warped into evil, and redeem them! Bad religion is not to be banished, but transformed.

To conclude, my answer to the question is this:
The violence we find in scripture describes God's relationship to a brutally violent world.
The violence we find in history often uses faith as a motivator.
We ought to confess to this and make amends.
In so doing we find the core of faith—forgiveness.
Faith expresses the ultimate, it comforts as few other things can, and Christ calls us to be religious in such a way that we can redeem religion.

A+A

15. Holocaust and Lutheranism
(Romans 13:1-7, Matthew 27:24-26, and John 18:33-36)

This second to last Sunday in our summer sermon series "8 questions from the pews" is a heavy one. The question is this: "What can Lutherans say about our complicity in the Holocaust?"

Part of me would simply like to respond with a time of silence.

But, I think, today calls for confession and understanding.

What can we say?
1. That the Lutheran tradition has within it a strain of submission to people in authority
2. a strain of anti-Judaism in it
Both of which make us complicit in the horror of the Holocaust.
3. Additionally, there was also a portion of the faith that resisted Nazism, but it wasn't enough and didn't go far enough.

Let us pray.

One aspect of the faith going all the way back to our beginnings is that common question "How do we relate to the state and the society in which we live?"

One tactic is to take Jesus' words "my kingdom is not of this world" to move all our concern in an otherworldly direction—to assume those things shaping day to day life here and now, are none of our business as Christians.

Similarly, and this is more the norm for us Lutherans, is to follow Paul's advice to the Romans—those in authority are there because God is the God of History, and therefore we ought to be good citizens of our country and not question authority.

Lutheranism's tendency to side with the powers that be, fits Luther's life experience—when there were death threats by the Pope and other Catholic officials it was the secular princes who kept him from trial and death. The state kept him alive and the reformation afloat, and he rightly thanked God for that
—not knowing the kind of murderous totalitarianism that was to come.

Now, Anti-Judaism is perhaps the original sin of Christianity. It was birthed out of that strange back and forth that lead to the cleaving of Judaism and Christianity. Rome called on Jews to denounce Christianity as a new cult—an innovation and therefore not exempt from Emperor worship,
and the Roman Empire called upon the early Christian movement to denounce Jews as rebels to be expelled from Rome and Jerusalem.

The debates and stories Jesus told within the Judaism of his time and Paul's description of "The Law" sounded much different coming from Gentile lips. It switched from being an inter-Jewish discussion to an antagonism from the outside.

Eventually Marcion, a Roman Christian, declared a separation between the "Jewish God" and the God revealed in Christ—and while he was condemned as a heretic, that did little to repair the widening breach between the two faiths.

Supersessionalism—the idea that the Church replaced Israel and the New Testament replaced the 10 commandments—still haunts the Christian heart to this very day.

In Nazi Germany this original sin was in full blossom—with wrongheaded arguments that Jesus was not a Jew and with renewed Marcionism—calling for the de-Judaizing of scripture.

Similarly, the unfortunate words attributed to the crowd in Matthew's telling of the passion, "His blood be on us and on our children," have been used to justify all kinds of horrible things done to the Jews—Pogroms in Poland, the Inquisition in Spain
—the charge of "Christ-Killer" comes from these words. In fact, so powerful a motivator were these words in past decades and centuries, that the panel on Lutheran-Jewish relations insisted, that "the New Testament ... must not be used as justification for hostility towards present-day Jews", and that "blame for the death of Jesus should not be attributed to Judaism or the Jewish people."—that is why on Good Friday you hear me talk a lot about Judeans and Religious Officials when I read the Passion account instead of the traditional translation "the Jews."

But, let's get a little more particular—what of Luther? At the age of 40 he wrote a tract against Dominican abuses of the Jewish populous entitled, "That Jesus Christ Was Born a Jew," in which he writes:
"Our fools, the popes, bishops, sophists, and monks—the crude asses—have treated the Jews in such a way that anyone who is truly a good Christian ought to become a Jew. If I was a Jew and heard such dolts and blockheads teach the Christian faith I would as soon be a wild boar as be a Christian."

If only he'd stopped there, but he did not. When he

was 60, a few years before his death, he wrote "On the Jews and Their Lies" a tract so vile that even his closest friend Melanchthon said it "reeked of the Inquisition."

In it he maps out a "solution" for what he calls the "Jewish problem" in Germany—that Synagogues and Jewish houses ought to be burnt, Talmuds taken, Rabbis forbidden to speak, safe passage on highways removed, Jewish property confiscated, and Jews made to be serfs on German farms until they choose to self-deport.

If this sounds similar to the Nazi "final solution," minus the gas chambers—there is a good reason for it—Luther's anti-Semitic writings were picked up quite whole-cloth by the National Socialists.

There were however some Lutherans who heard the pseudo-Theological claims of the Nazis such as:
"The New Word of God is found in the History of the German People."
"Jesus is not Savior but a Hero-Prophet for the Church just as Hitler is the Hero-Prophet of Germany."
And "You may only believe in the resurrection if you believe in the resurrection of Germany."
They heard these claims and took the entire Nazi program as an attack on the Church.

When most German Church-folk were asking the question, "Should the Nazi controlled Church be more Calvinist or Lutheran?" There was a movement called the Confessing Church, who believed the Nazis should not control the Church and responded with the Barman Declaration, which we will confess together in place of the Apostle's Creed in today's service.

One of those members of the Confessing Church, Reverend Doctor Dietrich Bonheoffer, responded to the situation in Nazi Germany by entering into a conspiracy to kill Hitler and smuggle German Jews to Switzerland. In fact one of the last orders of the Nazi High Command before they lost the control of German was "Bonheoffer must die." And indeed he was executed in the Flossenburg concentration camp on April 9th 1945

    I bring up these heroes not to absolve us, but to challenge us to hear God in the midst of societal noise and historical half-truths. Challenge us to hear the Gospel above the clangor of Culture, to hear always the cries of our common humanity.

    So, "What can Lutherans say about our complicity in the Holocaust?"

    Christianity's original sin Anti-Judaism, and Luther's tract "On the Jews and Their Lies" are part of a train of thought that leads to Auschwitz.

    The Lutheran hesitancy to challenge secular authorities ensured that resistance to, or even questioning of, "The Final Solution" was limited.

    Finally, I thank God that there were some who tapped other veins of our tradition—Theology of the Cross and Scripture Alone—and in so doing resisted Nazism and the Holocaust.

We mourn the majority's inaction and wrong actions, we remember the martyrs who died doing what was right, and we continue to pledge to the 20 million victims of the Nazi regime, especially the 6 million Jews, never again. Amen.

16. The End
(Mark 11:1-4, 11:15-22 and 13:24-31)

On this, the final Sunday in our summer sermon series "8 Question from the Pews," we end with a rather appropriate question... or rather an appropriate request "Talk about what 'the end' means."
To do this we'll:
1. Consider two meanings of the word
2. And look at what today's gospel readings from the Gospel of Mark look like in light of those two meanings of the word

Let us pray.

The End.
When we talk about it theologically, we often think about the book of Revelation, Millenialism of various sorts, the Late Great Planet Earth, and the Left Behind Series.
What all these things have in common is an assumption that the definition of "The End" we're using is "The conclusion" or "Termination." "Ceasing." "Stopping." A period or exclamation mark, as opposed to a comma or semi-colon.
And this is probably what the questioner meant.
They're likely wondering what it'll all be like when the earth ceases to exist, or this particular epoch, this particular time period, stops.

Yet, I would suggest another one of the 7 definitions of "End" is worth considering when we look at scripture— the end defined as "**Goal**." The end of something is **its direction**, where it is going.
By way of example, our Episcopal brothers and

sisters confess: "The Chief End of Man is to glorify God and to enjoy him forever."

So, instead of "The End" being a period, or point ending a line, it's an arrow pointing toward a goal.

Let's consider Mark's Gospel in light of these two meanings.

A more literalist reading of Mark's Gospel points us toward the first definition of End "The Passing away of heaven and earth," the evaporation of the world.

In this reading Jesus is warning us that at some unknown time there will be a period of cosmic darkness, and the Son of Man—this figure from the book of Daniel, will arrive and we ought to look for signs and keep awake so we know when it happens and are not caught unaware.

Some read this as pointing toward the destruction of the temple, or more commonly, as pointing toward the destruction of the world. In this case, they say, Jesus is telling us to look around and read everything as a sign, to be anxious for the coming cosmic thunderclap that will end it all.

But let's consider **option B**—the End as an arrow pointing toward a goal.

To do this we can look more particularly at a pattern in Mark's Gospel—**his dealing with fig trees.**

Yes, Fig trees, it might seem a weird place to go into order to talk about the end—with a plant... but Jesus himself describes the coming of The Son of Man as being announced like a fig tree announces summer.

So, let's consider the Fig Tree.

Jesus enters Jerusalem the first time, his humble act of riding a donkey, *which proclaims the kind of Kingdom we are called to*, is met with leaves galore—it at first seems that there is a fruitful acceptance of the Kingdom of God.

But, **at the gates of Jerusalem**, just outside the city limits, back in Bethany, Jesus sees the truth, writ large on that small Fig Tree, there are leaves but no fruit, and so he curses it. As in Jerusalem, so too the fig tree, both unfruitful.

Then he again passes the threshold between Bethany and Jerusalem and enters to see the Temple, and attacks it, turning tables expelling sellers, and mightily kicking out moneychangers.

And again he returns to Bethany, just outside of Jerusalem, he sees this fig tree again, this time withered.

Then, a third time, Jesus, in Jerusalem, declares that there will be a time of darkness in which the Son of Man will be reveled, he will be at the very gate of Jerusalem—at the threshold and his presence will be announced like a fig tree announces summer.

Then Jesus encourages us to stay awake for the Son of Man, for he might show up at:
evening,
midnight
cockcrow
or at dawn.

Again, lots of people see this as Jesus explaining what it will be like when the earth ceases to exist... but, what if this is a goal he is describing? What if it describes his Passion, Death, and Resurrection, and is telling us where we might find our Master?

After all, on two previous occasions the events in

Jerusalem paralleled the sign of the Fig Tree.

    The Son of Man is coming Jesus tells the high Priest—and then Jesus adds that, he, Jesus, is the Son of Man.
    We must keep alert, stay awake, to see him—look at the Disciples at Gethsemane, who fail to do so.
    That **evening**, the Last Supper, they meet the Son of Man in the breaking of the bread and the drinking of the wine.
    At **midnight** those in power are judged by the Son of Man, even as they put him on trial.
    When **the cock crows**, Peter makes a fateful choice and denies the Son of Man.
    At **dawn**, the women meet the resurrected Lord.

    What if the point of talking about the end is not some deathwatch for the world, or a waiting for everything to be over... what if instead the end is a goal, to stay awake that we might experience again the saving story of Jesus Christ's Life, Death, and Resurrection...
that we might trust in his resurrection,
recognize when we deny our Lord,
eschew the powers of this world that judge falsely,
meet our Lord in the Holy Meal of Communion,
be awake in prayer,
and confess to all that Jesus is our Lord.
A+A.

Year 3

17. Samson's Faith
(Judges 15:1-8 and Hebrews 11:29-40)

So, let me tell you about a guy! A real emblem of faith...
　　The **Philistines** had conquered the Israelites, and they needed someone to protect them from this new threat...
so God sent an angel to Samson's barren parents,
who promised them a child,
and made them swear an oath,
that Samson would never cut his hair, or be ritually impure, or drink strong drink.
　　This man, Samson, starts his ministry by marrying a...
Philistine...
you know, the people he was supposed to protect the Israelites from...
　　And he's wandering to his bachelor party, and along the way he has a run in with a lion and rips it in half.
　　Once at the bachelor party, he picks a fight with his future brother-in-laws, and kills a bunch of them.
　　His would-be father-in-law thinks this means the marriage is off,
and marries Samson's bride-to-be to the best man...
and then we come to today's story about the flaming foxes.
　　By this point, Samson's own people have decided he's *a little funny*, and a danger to himself and others...
so they turn him over to the **Philistine** authorities....
Once arrested he kills, and kills, and kills, and kills, until the Philistine forces are all gone and God offers him a cool drink of water.

Thirst satiated, he finds himself a prostitute in the city, and when his love shack is surrounded by an angry mob he hides out until midnight and then beats a hasty retreat,
carrying the city gates themselves off with him**, for the fun of it.**

Then he falls in love with Delilah, another **Philistine**, who he famously lies to about the source of his strength a couple of times, before he tells the truth,
which gets him **shorn** and **captured** and **blinded** and **bound**.

Then, in the final act, he's put between pillars of a house where sacrifices to the **Philistine** god Dagon were taking place
—all the leaders of the **Philistines** are giving thanks to Dagon for allowing them to capture Samson,
and Samson goes from weakness to strength and strains and pushes those pillars down
—killing everyone, including himself
—3,000 in all.

And that gets me to the first question in our 3-week sermon series "Questions from the Pews."
Today's question is:
"Why is Samson in the bible in the book of "Hebrews" as a man of faith?"

Let us pray

"Why is Samson in the bible in the book of "Hebrews" as a man of faith?"

Now, to begin with, we have to come to grips with the fact that *the Bible is a collection of books*
—**the bible is a library of books we believe point to the God we know in Jesus Christ.**

Stating the obvious,
not all books say the same thing,
they have different *focuses* and different *points*.
And today, at least to some extent, we're looking at two
books of the Bible that are *working at **cross-purposes**.*

One of the main point of the book of Judges is that
the system for ruling God's people after the death of Moses
and Joshua, was ineffective—it worked *very* poorly.
Essentially, you had 12 tribes living side-by-side, but
separate, other than when bad things happened,
at which point they would cry to God and a Judge
—a charismatic ruler
—would arise and unite the tribes and stop whatever bad
thing had befallen them.
The problem was, *with the exception of Deborah
and a few barely mentioned Judges*, most of these judges
were **deeply, and I mean DEEPLY, flawed individuals**
—*Jephthah* sacrificed his own daughter because he made a
dumb oath,
Barak was a coward,
Gideon and Micah made idols,
AbiMelek slaughtered his own brothers,
tribes warred against one another, culminating in the near
genocide of the tribe of Benjamin...
and as we see today, we also have hyped-up, sexed-up,
erratic, frat-boy Samson.
The point the book of Judges is making, is that *the
system is messed up*; a Davidic king is needed...

This is, however, not the point of Hebrews.
Hebrews is a sermon focused on giving **hope** to early
Christians facing persecution;
preaching to a Christian community where there are people

falling away,
because being Christian involves sacrifice
—the preacher is telling us that, in the face of persecution, we need to **trust in the unseen things of God**, *just like the faithful who came before did*. Though it doesn't always seem like it...
God is in relationship with us,
God has made a promise to us,
and we ought to **trust in that promise**,
just as God was in relationship with folk throughout the bible.

So, on one hand the book of Judges goes out of its way to show that many of the Judges are **flawed**,
on the other, Hebrews points to their **faithfulness**.

And that's where the preacher is going—he is giving concrete examples of people living out their faith in times of trouble, so that his listeners can do the same.
He mentions Samson in this list of people—and it is a little unclear why.
Is it because he his parents "**obtained promises**" from God through his birth?
Is it because he "**shuts the mouth of lions**" by tearing one to shreds?
Is it because he "**won strength out of weakness**" there at the end of his story?

Or, maybe, the list the preacher gives, is of people both succeeding and failing,
sinners and saints
—faithful in so far as God has been faithful to them.
Yes, enduring as best they can, but ultimately **relying on God**, relying on the ongoing **relationship** God has with

them.
     Relying on the reality that even **an Idol maker like Gideon**,
a Coward like Barak,
a Shmuck like Samson,
a fool like Jephthah,
and **ALL** the rest
—relying on the reality that even ***THEY*** found a gracious God,
a faithful God,
a God who kept faith with them even at their ugliest.
    So, **"why is Samson in the bible in the book of "Hebrews" as a man of faith?"**
Because God is faithful.
God walked with **him of all people**
and
God walks with **us** even on our **darkest and dumbest day**.
    We can't always see that, like the early Christians the Preacher of Hebrews is preaching to,
we can be so put down by the things we can see,
that we sacrifice our hope in the invisible Grace of God,
and we can fall away.
    So, let me remind you, if God can be faithful to Samson,
gracious to Samson,
in relationship with Samson
—he surely is with you all of your days,
generously,
graciously,
faithfully. A+A

18. Easy Sin, Hard Faith
(Romans 7:14-25 and Luke 23:34)

Today's question, the 2nd one in our 3 week sermon series "Questions from the Pews" is this: **"Why is sin so easy and being a Christian so hard?"**
There is a lot packed into this singular question. What is sin? For example, are we talking little s—foibles and folly, or big S, a controlling power?
What does it mean to be a human being? Are we inclined to evil, made that way, corrupted, or what?
What does it mean, as well, to be a Christian? Are we talking about being polite—"*That was a right Christian thing you did today.*" Or about community values, or about a relationship with Christ?
But, before I venture too far off into the weeds with all this, I'll give a simple answer to the question **"Why is sin so easy and being a Christian so hard?"**
Sin is easy because we're mortals / infected by Sin. Being Christian is both impossible *and* easy.
Prayer

Sin is easy because we're **mortals**
 infected by Sin.
>   We're **mortal**.
This has two very practical implications. 1. We're afraid of death. 2. We have a limited understanding of the world around us.

We're **afraid** of death—not always obviously, but so much of what we do is a denial of this firm reality. Everything from...
societal obsession with youth culture
to the way we talk euphemistically about funerals

to the general disregard we show for those generations who will live after we ourselves are dead.
    The shadow of death that looms over our lives clouds our judgment, and makes us more closed fisted than we ought to be, more concerned about self and self-preservation than is sane for a species such as our own.

    Death, also, is the ultimate **blinder**.
Our limited nature
—that we can only experience and know so much
—makes all of our choices unsteady and ambiguous.
Our viewpoint, both as individuals and as a species, is so limited that when the Unlimited One showed up,
when Jesus showed up,
we crucified him.
We were unable to recognize the one who recognized us from before we were born, from before creation was created!
 It is as Jesus says from the cross, **"They know not what they do."**

We're **infected** by sin.
    Sin isn't simply individual accidents,
or bad habits,
or even sins plural,
instead it is a force, a power that controls us
—Sin,
singular
with a capital S.
    As Paul writes in Romans, Sin has captured us, and not only us, but the Law itself. The Law of God, a good thing, is used to a bad end.
So too we, good and beautiful creatures created in the

image of God, are used to a bad end.
Think of it:
Cowardice overshoots **courage** and becomes **rashness**.
Selfishness overshoots **love** and becomes **enabling**.

Paul describes this situation we're in as being captured,
being sold into slavery,
so we can't do the very thing we wish to do, because our vile master, Sin, has control over us.
Or, thinking of a more up-to-date description
—Sin is an addiction we can not break.
Or as I like to think of it, Sin is an infection
—a disease that has overcome us all,
a cancer that has transformed good cells into destructive ones
—using the best as the worst.
Our individual sinful actions are simply symptoms of the wider disease,
a contagion raging through the whole world to such an extent that we don't even notice we're all infected.
A parasite plugged into each one of us that will not let go.
Why can't I quit sin, because it's inside of me
… just as an infected person can't simply stop infecting, because it is inside of them. More than that, it has infected the whole earth and holds it in its sway.

Yes, Sin is easy because we're mortals, blinded and made stingy by death.
Yes, Sin is easy because we're infected by Sin, captured and surrounded by its power.

<u>Being Christian is both impossible and easy.</u>
If being Christian is about being good,

about healing ourselves from the infection of sin,
of freeing ourselves from the slaver sin,
or becoming a dry drunk by not acting on our addictions
and at the same time not dealing with the underlying problems
—treating symptoms but not diseases
—then Christianity is impossible.
    If being a Christian is an action, a disposition,
something we do and we are...
synonymous with nice,
or clean,
or some other virtue,
some symptom of church attendance or something
—the little c christian to balance out the little s-plural sins,
then it is impossible,
for we can neither will ourselves to be Christ-like,
 nor push past sin,
nor barrel-roll away from death.

    But, if being Christian is about God acting for us,
then it is not impossible, nor even hard, it is easy.
Think of Samson who we encountered last week—a schmuck among schmucks, yet God was faithful, being a person of faith was easy because God stuck with him.
    Or look at Paul in Romans... he reaches a breaking point—the impossibility of this life of sin we live:
"I delight in the Law of God—but I make war against myself!
    "I battle sin on the outside, but am already captured by sin on the inside!
    "Who will save a wretch like me?
    "Who can rescue one such as me? I, in whom death dwells?"
    To which he responds with this glorious affirmation,

"Thanks be to God through Jesus Christ our Lord."
He throws his hands up in despair at the impossibility of it all, but then flips his palms up in a posture of praise!
It was that simple,
that easy
—Christ Jesus did it for him.
In the face of death,
the curdling of our generosity,
Christ opens his hands to all from the cross.
In the face of death and the way it blinds us,
Christ intercedes with his father, "They don't know what they're doing, forgive them!"
Enslaved by Sin,
Christ pays our debt and frees us.
Addicted to Sin,
Christ walks with us and digs deep, dealing with symptom and disease.
Infected by Sin,
Christ destroys that parasite and frees us to be who we are. A+A

19. Justice
(Exodus 23:1-9, Micah 6:6-8, and Luke 4:16-21)

As we reach this, the third and final question from the pews, the end of this summer sermon series, we reach a question heavy with history and packed with political import even today.

The question is: "What is God's justice? Is God concerned with Justice? How should we act to be in accord with God's justice?"

The short answer is, God's justice is about making all things right. God is deeply concerned with Justice, in fact, it is mentioned explicitly in scripture 173 times and words related to it are mentioned nearly 2,000 times! Finally, we ought to act with justice.

In order to get a sense of what justice might mean to God, and to us, it is worth looking at the broad scope of scripture and how justice is expressed therein. So, take a peek at what Justice looks like in the Torah, Prophets, and Writings of the Old Testament and how Justice is found in Jesus. Then we'll think for a moment what that means for God, and for human beings.
Prayer

In the first five books of the Old Testament, the Torah, we find God's people newly freed from slavery
—one of the ultimate acts of injustice,
and shaping their society with an eye toward **justice**.
Making right that which is wrong.
But what does that look like?
1. **Impartiality**,
2. **fair** distribution of land and forgiveness of debt,
3. and all of this is done in an **expansive** way.

Justice looked like **impartiality** on the part of those in power. Courts and kings and everyone else was to govern fairly, treating everyone **equally**,
especially those who had the least power,
widows, orphans, and the like.
Now, you could rightly say, "hold up there Pastor" **Equally** and **especially,** don't go together
—either you treat everyone the same, or not... ...but as we read in our first lesson today, the author of Exodus was well aware that
the **least of these** are **least likely** to get a fair shake, most likely to loose a lawsuit because the deck is stacked against them,
most likely to bear the brunt of bribery and corruption.
So, justice involves the rules of society to be fair for all,
but <u>especially</u> for the least of us.

One of the most radical aspects of Israelite society, one that some scholars think was so impractical **that it was never actually practiced,** was the idea of a Jubilee year. A year when everything, *especially land*, reverted back to its original owner...
This is a strange proposition when you think of it, simultaneously leftist and reactionary!
The idea is every 49 years everyone returns to the land that their tribe received from God as laid out in the Torah and the book of Joshua.
Think of it!
You're from the tribe of Dan in the north, but you've lived down south in Judah your whole life and prospered well, you've accrued a bunch of land and wealth, and then year 49 hits. All of a sudden you've got to take your family and move north to Dan, and live on a tiny plot of land there, giving up all you own to the members of the tribe of Judah

who have ancestral right to it.
    Think if this was the case today, where did your family originally settle? Imagine having to leave everything you have and trek back there with your family and start over again.
    The Jubilee year recognized that over time power and wealth **accrue** to <u>some</u> families more than to <u>others</u>, and if you're one of the others,
dug into a hole,
digging out becomes harder the longer you are down there...
and so, every 49 years there was a **reset button**—like the one for the router of your wireless, you poke a pen tip into it and boom,
debts forgiven,
slaves freed,
land restored.

    Finally, we see in the Torah that the promise of justice is not solely for citizens of the Land, but also for those passing through the land or immigrating to the land. Justice, for sojourners and immigrants,
resident aliens and even enemies!
Justice, for all!

    In the Torah the community that came out of slavery in Egypt is encouraged to be **<u>just</u>** by being **fair**,
especially to the least of these,
by **resetting** social standing every generation,
and **expanding out** this sense of justice beyond those within its immediate borders.
    This understanding of Justice swells in the books of the Prophets.
Prophets look around at their society and recognize that so

often the ideals of the Exodus have been abandoned,
that Justice is for **just us**,
that debts have been **accrued so much** that the poor go without footwear and coats on cold nights,
that simple ideas of **equal treatment** aren't practiced **anywhere**.
If all that wasn't bad enough, the people try to cover up all of their societal sins with religious ritual
—*look, I made a burnt offering, I even did it in a big way*
—*our country is so very religious!*
    To which the prophets of every age reply, "do justice! Love kindness! Walk humbly with your God!"

    As for the Writings, the focus is on how a Just society creates **individual good**, they explored how Justice created what Philosophers might call the good life.
If you act unjustly it is unwise and leads to death.
If you act Justly you also act wisely, in a life giving way.

    As for the Gospel, the good news of Jesus Christ, listen to Jesus' <u>mission statement</u>:
'The Spirit of the Lord is upon me,
  because he has anointed me
    to bring good news to the **poor**.
He has sent me to proclaim release to the **captives**
  and recovery of sight to the **blind**,
    to let the **oppressed** go free,
to proclaim **the year of the Lord's favor**.'
    Jesus embodies God's justice. His presence among us is good news, **especially** for the poor, captive, blind, oppressed, he is proclaiming a **Jubilee year** for them all
—a new start for them,
for all of us!
    Yes, God showing up in Jesus is an example of

justice
—<u>that same type of Justice God has been about since the exodus</u>.
Justice for <u>all</u>, *but especially for the least of these.*
A leveling—think of Mary's Song in which *thrones are thrown down and the lowly are lifted up.*
An expansion of those who fall under the Reign of God—the citizenship among the saints is expanded, most noticeably in Paul's mission to the Gentiles.

So, what does this all mean for God and for us humans?
Judging from the descriptions of God's concerns found in scripture, we can be assured God is concerned about **Justice** and that part of God making all things right involves the 3-fold pattern of justices I've described.
*How should we act...***there is the rub, right?**
We cling to the Just and Merciful acts of God, and then act as if we don't just believe them in our head and heart, but with our hands and our whole self as well. Working in **our own selves** to make it true, and **among our whole society** to make it so.
It is a right and Christian thing to call for fairness and focus on those who bear the brunt of injustice.
There was a Christian movement back in the year 2000 to make it a Jubilee year in which the richest countries in the world forgave the debts of the poorest countries in the world—you might remember the musician Bono of U2 heading it up this effort—this was faithful to the original intent of the Jubilee year.
Christianity ought to always be peeking through the cracks that our culture creates so that we might see those left out, and invite them in and act in such a way that their full dignity might be upheld. A+A

Made in the USA
Charleston, SC
29 October 2016